Michael B. Barry

THE GREEN DIVIDE

An Illustrated History of the Irish Civil War

Andalus Press

Published by Andalus Press
7 Frankfort Avenue, Rathgar, Dublin 6
Ireland
www.andalus.ie
info@andalus.ie

ISBN 978-0-9560383-6-4

By the same author:
Across Deep Waters, Bridges of Ireland
Restoring a Victorian House
Through the Cities, the Revolution in Light Rail
Homage to al-Andalus, the Rise and Fall of Islamic Spain
Tales of the Permanent Way, Stories from the Heart of Ireland's Railways
Victorian Dublin Revealed, the Remarkable Legacy of Nineteenth-Century Dublin
Fifty Things to do in Dublin
Dublin's Strangest Tales (with Patrick Sammon)
Beyond the Chaos, the Remarkable Heritage of Syria

Jacket Images
Front flap: bottom image, Diarmuid O'Connor. Front cover: top left, Risteárd Mulcahy; top right, George Morrison; map, National Library of Ireland; bottom left, National Archives of Ireland; bottom right, Central Catholic Library. Back cover: melange of images – National Library of Ireland; George Morrison; Mercier Press and Dún Laoghaire-Rathdown Libraries. Back flap: author photograph, Veronica Barry; bottom image, Mercier Press and Dún Laoghaire-Rathdown Libraries.

Jacket design by Anú Design
Maps and book design by Michael B. Barry
Vignettes at chapter headings by Veronica Barry

Printed by Printer Trento S.r.l. Italy

Contents

FOR OLIVIA ALEXANDRINE BARRY

Acknowledgements

This book benefited from the help, insights and scholarship of many kind people. Thanks are due especially to: George Morrison; John Dorney; Risteárd Mulcahy; Liz Gillis; Dr Brian Kirby, Irish Capuchin Provincial Archives; Niall Bergin, Kilmainham Archives and Diarmuid O'Connor.

The following were very helpful to me: Tony McGettigan; Frank Twomey; Tommy Mooney; Cormac O'Malley; John R. Bowen; Michael Forde; Tony Redmond; Tom Harrington; Cecelia Lynch O'Carroll; Moss Hannon; Joseph Scanlon; John Ward-McQuaid; Joe Maxwell; Geraldine McCarthy; Donal King; Michael O'Connor 'Scarteen'; Ivan Lennon; Professor Frank Imbusch; John Kirby; Donal MacLynn; Martin O'Dwyer; Oliver Doyle; David Byrne; Nick West; Liam Brennan; Michael Hinch, Irish Independent; Dr Margarita Cappock, Dublin City Gallery; Sharon O'Donovan, Mercier Press; Nigel Curtin, Dún Laoghaire-Rathdown Libraries; Honora Faul, Bernie Metcalfe, Glenn Dunne, National Library of Ireland; Mario Corrigan, James Durney, Kildare Library and Arts Services; Seamus Helferty, UCD Archives; Sergeant Charles Walsh, Curragh Military Museum; Teresa Whitington, Central Catholic Library; Peter Beirne, Clare County Library; Michael Fitzgerald, Waterford County Museum; Finbarr Connolly, National Museum of Ireland; Brian Hodkinson, Limerick City Archives; Commandant Padraic Kennedy, Hugh Beckett, Lisa Dolan, Noelle Grothier, Military Archives, Cathal Brugha Barracks; Gerry Curran, Courts Service; Aideen Ireland, National Archives of Ireland; Tony O'Shaughnessy, Clifton Flewitt, Irish Railway Records Society; Gregg Ryan, Iarnród Éireann; Michael Lynch, Kerry Library Archives; Malachy Gillen, Sligo Library Archives; Westport Heritage Centre; George Rugg, University of Notre Dame and Mary Clarke, Dr Enda Leaney, Maire Kennedy, Eithne Massey, Dublin City Library & Archive.

I wish to particularly note the assistance and kindness of Shane MacThomáis, of Glasnevin Museum, and remember him. He is sadly missed.

Veronica Barry and Patrick Sammon laboured mightily in the verbal vineyards in an endeavour to put order on my undulating words. If the result is not of veritable verbal vintage material, it is my fault.

Illustration Credits

Images on the specified pages are courtesy of the following (abbreviations for top, bottom, left, middle, right, respectively, are: t, b, l, m, r):

British National Archives: 148t. Irish Capuchin Provincial Archives, Dublin: 37b; 38b; 45b; 54b; 80; 104t 116t; 121b; 125b; 156t; 161bl; 161br. Central Catholic Library: 14t; 17l; 18b; 152b; 160bl; 167b. ClydeMaritime Forums: 21bl. David Byrne: 27b. Department of Rare Books & Special Collections, Hesburgh Libraries of Notre Dame University: 114b. Diarmuid O'Connor: 34b; 41b; 42t; 78t; 174bl. Donal McCarron, Joe Maxwell & Irish Indpendent: 88t; Donal MacLynn: 154b. Dublin City Gallery The Hugh Lane: 123b. Dublin City Library & Archive: 34t; 36b; 43b; 45t; 51t; 53b; 56b; 126br. Frank Twomey: 148b. George Morrison: 13t;14b; 29t; 58t; 62b; 70t; 72b; 73; 76; 77; 93t; 98t; 100t; 101t; 118tl; 140t; 157t; 163t; 179t; 181t; 182. Geraldine McCarthy: 162br. Iarnród Éireann: 128bl; 135br. iCollector.com: 27 tr. Irish Independent: 86b; irishmedals.org: 166 bl. Irish Railway Record Society: 104b; 128br; 130t; 131b; 132; 133; 134; 135t; 137b; 140b; 142b; 143b. John R. Bowen: 114m. John Ward-McQuaid: 149 bl. Kerry Library Archives (and the Fionán Lynch family): 67b; 126t. Kildare Library and Arts Services: 178b. Kilmainham Gaol Archives: 17b r; 22b; 23b; 48b; 160mr; 160br; 171bl. Liam Brennan: 138t. Limerick City Archives (courtesy of George Imbusch collection): 62t & 63 t; 64t & 65 t; 66t & 67t. Limerick City Archives: 61b; 66b; 68b; 156bl. Martin O'Dwyer: 172b. Max Decals Publications Ltd: 86t. Mercier Press & Dún Laoghaire-Rathdown Libraries: 16b; 21t; 36t; 40; 47; 51b; 53t; 55b; 56t; 57; 58b; 84b; 144t; 175br. Michael O'Connor 'Scarteen': 95b. Military Archives, Cathal Brugha Barracks: 30bl; 30br; 39b; 43t; 82t; 84t; 91b; 105b; 108b; 109b; 129; 130b; 152t; 176mr. Military Museum, Curragh: 27; 100b; 118b; 119; 121t. Moss Hannon: 176bl. National Archives of Ireland and the Director NAI: 15t (TSCH/5/2002/5/1); 42b (will of M. C. Fitzmaurice); 83b (TSCH/3/S14205); 90t (TSCH/3/S1385); 157b (TSCH/3S1369/14); 173b (PG / IFS, File 48 B "Captured Documents"). National Library of Ireland: 15b; 19b; 20t; 21br; 24; 25; 28; 29b; 32t; 35b; 44t; 48t; 49; 50; 54t; 60; 63b; 69b; 70b; 71t; 72t; 75; 79; 85; 87m; 93b; 97; 98b; 99t; 103t; 106 ;107; 108t; 112t; 120; 123t; 124; 125t; 126bl; 128t; 131t; 136 ;146b; 147t; 153t; 158; 159t; 161t; 164t; 165t; 174br; 178t; 183; 184t; 185b. National Museum of Ireland & Risteárd Mulcahy: 12t. National Museum of Ireland: 39t; 175bl. Nick West: 135bl; 137tl; 144br. Risteárd Mulcahy: 116b; 153b; 181b. UCD Archives: 18t & 19t; 20b; 109t. Waterford County Museum: 78b; 147b; 185t. Wikimedia Commons: 27tl – Rama; 83t – Avalokitesvara.

Images on pages 12b;13b; 16tr; 55t; 65b; 87b; 112b; 160ml ;162t; 162bl; 162b and 180 are from the *Illustrated London News*; images on pages 54m; 71b and 146t are from *Dublin Opinion*.

All other photographs and maps are copyright Michael B. Barry © 2014.

Every effort has been made to establish copyright, but if a copyright holder wishes to bring an error to the notice of the publishers, then an appropriate acknowledgement will be made in any subsequent edition.

Chronology 1922-23

1922

3 January	Dáil meets and resumes Treaty debate.
7 January	With 64 votes in favour, 57 against, Dáil approves Treaty.
10 January	De Valera and other supporters leave Dáil. Griffith elected President.
14 January	'Southern Parliament' meets and sets up Provisional Government.
31 January	New Provisional Government army sets up HQ at Beggar's Bush Barracks.
5 March	Stand-off between pro- and anti-Treaty forces at Limerick.
14 March	Public meeting in Cork with Michael Collins disrupted by anti-Treaty supporters.
17 March	De Valera makes a speech warning about the Volunteers having "to wade through Irish blood" at meeting in Thurles.
26 March	IRA Convention at Mansion House repudiates Treaty and appoints Executive.
29 March	Anti-Treaty IRA destroys presses of *Freemans Press* after 'misleading reports'.
29 March	Capture of ship *Upnor* by Cork IRA and seizure of arms.
14 April	Takeover of Four Courts, in the early hours, by anti-Treaty forces.
16 April	Despite proclamation banning meeting in Sligo by IRA, Griffith speaks, supported by large number of pro-Treaty troops.
2 May	After several days of jostling for position, firing breaks out between both sides in Kilkenny. Two hundred troops arrive from Beggars Bush and there is an assault on Republicans ensconced in Kilkenny Castle. The castle is captured. Envoys arrive to impose peace.
4 May	A joint committee representing both sides meets in Dublin and establishes a truce.
20 May	De Valera and Collins announce pact for election planned for June.
5 June	British forces shell Provisional Government army positions in Pettigo, Co. Donegal.
14 June	Collins, at election meeting in Cork, repudiates the election pact.
16 June	Election in 26 Counties. Results are: 58 pro-Treaty seats; 36 anti-Treaty; 34 Labour and others.
22 June	Sir Henry Wilson assassinated in London.
26 June	JJ O'Connell, Deputy Chief of Staff, Provisional Government army, is kidnapped and held at Four Courts.
28 June	Four Courts garrison issued with demand to surrender at 3:40 am. Artillery bombardment starts shortly afterwards.
29 June	Following continuous shelling, pro-Treaty troops storm breaches in Four Courts.
30 June	Large explosion at Four Courts, followed by several others. Garrison surrenders.
30 June	Republicans have set up in Dublin city centre area. Fighting intensifies around the 'Block' in Upper Sackville St.
5 July	After days of fighting, the 'Block' is in ruins. Cathal Brugha emerges fighting, is shot and mortally wounded.
6 July	Republican forces have assembled in Blessington, but disperse several days later on the approach of large numbers of pro-Treaty forces.
11 July	Following a truce in Limerick, clashes begin after the arrival of pro-Treaty reinforcements.
12 July	A 'War Council' of three is created by Michael Collins.
20 July	General Prout and his forces take Waterford from the Republicans.
20 July	Anti-Treaty forces withdraw from Limerick after barracks are shelled.
24 July	Provisional Government forces land at Westport.
1 August	Harry Boland shot and mortally wounded during early-morning raid at hotel in Skerries where he was staying.
2 August	Pro-Treaty troops land at Fenit and take Tralee.
5 August	Kilmallock captured by pro-Treaty forces.
8 August	Provisional Government army under General Dalton lands at Passage West.
10 August	Cork City captured by pro-Treaty forces.
11 August	Pro-Treaty forces under Commandant O'Connor 'Scarteen' land at Kenmare and take the town.
12 August	Arthur Griffith dies of a cerebral haemorrhage.

22 August	Michael Collins, on tour of West Cork, is ambushed and shot at Bealnablath.
25 August	WT Cosgrave is appointed Chairman of the Provisional Government.
9 September	Third Dáil meets.
9 September	Republicans attack and retake Kenmare. Commandant O'Connor 'Scarteen'and his brother are shot dead.
16 September	Seven pro-Treaty soldiers (including Col-Commandant Tom Keogh) are killed by a trap mine near Macroom.
20 September	Pro-Treaty troops mount a sweep through the Sligo area. Six Republicans are captured and shot dead on Benbulben.
10 October	Pastoral issued by Irish Roman Catholic Bishops condemning the anti-Treaty side.
15 October	Public Safety Act becomes effective. It includes powers for military courts to issue death sentences.
17 October	Formation of Republican government in opposition with de Valera as President of the Republic.
25 October	Constitution of the Irish Free State enacted by the Dáil.
October	Railway Protection, Repair & Maintenance Corps set up to defend the railways and repair damage.
10 November	Erskine Childers arrested at Annamoe, Co. Wicklow and charged with possession of a revolver.
17 November	Four young Republicans are executed for possession of weapons.
24 November	Childers, sentenced to death, is executed at Beggar's Bush Barracks.
30 November	Liam Lynch, IRA Chief of Staff, issues general order to assassinate those who appoved the Public Safety Act.
6 December	Irish Free State comes into being.
7 December	Seán Hales, pro-Treaty TD, is assassinated in Dublin.
8 December	Four Republican prisoners (O'Connor, Mellows, McKelvey, Barrett) are executed in Mountjoy as a reprisal for the killing of Hales.
10 December	House of prominent pro-Treaty supporter Sean McGarry is burnt at Philipsburgh Avenue in Dublin. His seven-year-old son, Emmet, dies of burns.
13 December	After seizing Carrick-on-Suir, Tom Barry leads a successful thrust by the anti-Treaty IRA and captures Thomastown and surrounding area, before withdrawing to Tipperary.

1923

13 January	WT Cosgrave's house in Rathfarnham is burnt down. In January and February similar widespread action is taken against pro-Treaty supporters.
9 February	After being captured in January, Liam Deasy, Officer Commanding First Southern Division, IRA, issues call to his comrades for immediate and unconditional surrender.
11 February	Thomas O'Higgins (father of Minister of Justice, Kevin) is shot dead during an attack to set his house on fire.
18 February	IRA leader Dinny Lacy shot in action at the Glen of Aherlow.
6 March	Six National Army soldiers killed at Knocknagoshel Co. Kerry after being lured to a trap mine.
7 March	Nine Republican prisoners are brought to Ballyseedy, near Tralee, tied together and blown up by a mine. Eight die, one escapes.
7 March	Four Republican prisoners are blown up by a mine at Countess Bridge, Killarney.
12 March	Five Republican prisoners are taken from Baghaghs workhouse near Caherciveen and blown up by a mine.
14 March	Four Republicans executed at Drumboe, Co Donegal.
26 March	Meeting of IRA Executive in Nire Valley, Co. Waterford votes narrowly in favour of continuing the war.
10 April	Liam Lynch and party, en route to reconvened IRA Executive meeting, flee up Crohan West in the Knockmealdowns to escape a sweep by a large force of Free State troops. Lynch is shot and dies that evening.
16 April	Siege of Republicans begins at Clashmealcon caves, North Kerry.
24 May	Frank Aiken, the new Chief of Staff, IRA, issues orders to cease fire and to dump arms.
20 July	Free State Government sends a request to the British that the Boundary Commission be set up.
15 August	De Valera attends a Sinn Féin meeting in Ennis for the General Election called for later in August and is arrested.
27 August	In the General Election, the anti-Treaty party, Sinn Féin wins 44 seats; the pro-Treaty party, Cumann na nGaedheal wins 63; while the Labour Party and others win 46.
13 October	A mass hunger strike in Mountjoy Gaol by Republican prisoners spreads across the other places of internment. It fizzles out a little over six weeks later. Prisoners are gradually released over following months, a process that continues up to mid-1924.

Introduction

Cogadh carad, caoi namhad
Proverb: only the common enemy gains when there is a fight among friends.

The Irish Civil War was a pivotal event in the foundation of the modern Irish State. However, few of the participants discussed it afterwards. Its history was not taught in any comprehensive way until recently. Among the general populace there is an awareness of what happened, but not much knowledge.

Surprisingly, there is no official count of casualties in the Irish Civil War. Estimates have fluctuated widely – from, at the lower, more reliable end, around 1,400 deaths (made up of 350 Republicans, 730 National Army and 300 civilians) to around 4,000. Whatever the real figure, the events of 1922-23 come within the Uppsala Conflict Program definition of a 'war' – at least 1,000 battle-related deaths in a year. It was a small war, but includes many layers of complexity.

There exists a multitude of books on the subject, including the outstanding *Green against Green* by Michael Hopkinson, as well as, in the illustrated genre, George Morrison's *The Irish Civil War* and recently, Liz Gillis' *Revolution in Dublin.* Many recent books focusing on local aspects of the conflict, the Mercier series in particular, have added immensely to the understanding of events.

With the general reader in mind, I decided it would be worthwhile to prepare a book that showed the main events of the conflict in an easily-accessible manner, using images selected for their relevance and composition. I have been fortunate to be able to use images such as the extraordinary Imbusch panoramic photographs as well as those of the railways from the Irish Railway Record Society and Iarnród Éireann collections. (Many people will be surprised at the extent of the destruction wreaked on the rail network, which is not widely known.) I juxtapose the old with the new – present-day photographs of locations where significant events took place. There is detail as well: documents and other artefacts. All are accompanied by informative captions, which I hope will add to the reader's understanding of the events of 1922-23. Throughout the story of the war, I have ventilated some of the atrocities on both sides, and I hope I have done so in an even-handed manner.

In the course of preparing this book, I was privileged to be in contact with relatives of some of the protagonists. While across the country there are still undoubtedly seams of bitterness over the Civil War, I was impressed, when talking to those whose family members had been killed or injured, to hear them recount their stories, with dignity and in measured tones.

There are memorials all over Ireland to the fallen of the Republican side – the most impressive by far is the Ballyseedy memorial by Yann Goulet. Plaques and many crosses (the Celtic cross seems *de rigueur*) are plentiful. Yet paradoxically, there are very few memorials to the Free State dead. Busts of Collins abound and the Tom Keogh memorial in Knockananna is notable, but there is little else.

I have tried to reflect the context, viewpoints and events that propelled both sides towards war. Fairness demands care with the nomenclature used for the participants. Piaras Béaslaí issued instructions on behalf of the Provisional Government to the press in July 1922 that the anti-Treaty forces, whom he called 'irregulars', must be referred to as 'bands' or 'armed men' and not as 'forces' or 'troops'. In this book, instead, I propose to use accurate and, it is my hope, understandable names. For the anti-Treaty side I use such terms as 'anti-Treaty forces', 'IRA' or 'Republicans'. (In using the latter I do not mean to imply that those on the pro-Treaty side were not republican; in reality the majority were for the long-term goal of a Republic but they had chosen to take the pragmatic road of accepting the Treaty in the meantime.) For the pro-Treaty side, it is a little more confusing, as they also termed themselves as IRA well into 1922. I use, variously, terms such as: 'pro-Treaty forces'; the 'National Army'; the 'army of the Provisional Government' (which became the army of the Free State on 6 December 1922).

The 'Irish Republic', as proclaimed in 1916, had acquired an extraordinary lustre. From the times of Wolfe Tone, the Fenians and the IRB, the lustre of the concept had been burnished by the sacrifice of 1916, and the setting up that Republic was the objective of most in the struggle for independence. However, there was only a vague awareness of what a 'Republic' might actually mean. This strong (but rather shallow in another sense) adherence to the 'Republic' was to collide with the atavism of the British Empire as evidenced by Lloyd George and his colleagues during the Treaty negotiations. Brought up in a narrow, privileged, world where monarchy and the supremacy of the British Empire (then sliding downwards from its apogee) were a *sine qua non*, the British negotiators could not understand the dangerous concept of total freedom for a neighbouring small nation and certainly not for a 'Republic'. While minor details were negotiated, the British did not give an inch on the issue of membership of the British Empire and or the oath of faithfulness to its King. The acceptance of the oath to the king of the ancient enemy (in reality, the oath was not as severe as generally perceived – it was to be 'faithful' to the King rather than to give 'allegiance') was a bitter pill that most of the IRA could not swallow. On the other hand, the offer of limited independence rather than Lloyd George's threat of "immediate and terrible war" (it probably would have been terrible), persuaded Collins, Griffith and others to take a more pragmatic route as evidenced by Collins' comment about the Treaty as being a "stepping-stone to the Republic."

The Civil War was not a simple black-and-white scenario of democrats who were pro-Treaty versus non-democrats who were anti-Treaty. The June 1922 General Election was not held in a truly democratic atmosphere: it was conducted against the coercive backround of the British threat of war if the Treaty was not accepted. As there was a prior election pact, the anti-Treaty side expected a coalition arrangement after the election. In addition, Collins' seemingly unilateral declaration in July 1922 of a War Council (composed of pro-Treaty former IRA leaders) stretched the concept of democracy and tilted the civil-military balance of the Provisional Government towards a military one, albeit briefly.

The seizure of the Four Courts, in the heart of Dublin, by the non-compromising wing of the IRA was a visible gesture of defiance to the Provisional Government, then at its most fragile. The pressure to intervene came to boiling point with demands for action from the British Cabinet, which, in a state of agitation after the Wilson assassination, had immediately ordered British forces to attack the Four Courts, only to be dissuaded by General Macready, their Commander-in-Chief in Ireland. The kidnapping of the Deputy Chief of Staff of the Provisional Government army proved to be the tipping point, and the hastily-planned bombardment of the Four Courts began.

On the anti-Treaty side, there had been no strategic planning in the event of conflict. In the early days the Republicans set up in containable, easily besieged, locations (examples include the Four Courts, crammed with much of the senior leadership, and the 'Block'). With the benefit of hindsight, one could estimate that the only time they could have won the war was in the early days of the Dublin fighting, when they could have flooded Dublin with thousands of fighters and overpowered the Provisional Government army, then relatively smaller in numbers of troops. Intense set-piece battles in Dublin, which favoured the pro-Treaty side with its artillery and armoured vehicles, were followed by similar actions in the city of Limerick and the region around it.

After the southern landings, the anti-Treaty side resorted to guerrilla encounters, coupled with attacks on the soft targets of railways and roads, disastrous for the economy. The execution of captured Republicans was ruthless and has, understandably, been given a high profile in books on the Civil War. However, the continuous sniping and trap-mine attacks on the pro-Treaty troops resulted in a continuous death toll. Estimates of the war casualties indicate that there were more National Army deaths than Republican, by a ratio of around two to one.

Looked at from GHQ in Portobello Barracks in July 1922, it must have seemed a daunting task. The south-west of the country was solidly in anti-Treaty hands. In some other parts, there was a patchwork, alternating between anti- and pro-Treaty control. To win such a war needed a ruthless, methodical mind. Luckily for the pro-Treaty side, the right man was in the right place. General Richard Mulcahy proceeded to plan and prosecute the war in a systematic manner, making the best of his army, most of whose soldiers were raw but whose numbers were rapidly increasing, and which had the benefit of plentiful military *matériel*, provided by the ever-watchful Great Power across the water.

"Give me lucky generals", said Napoleon. Mulcahy was lucky, given that his series of amphibious landings, all successful, could have gone disastrously wrong. On the other side, the IRA comprised a confederation of strong local leaders. Each, to a lesser or greater degree, conducted a reactive war of harassing the Provisional Government army, (which, by the end of September 1922, was largely in command of the towns and barracks). The IRA Chief of Staff, Liam Lynch, was a diligent and honourable man, but the question must be raised: had he the necessary level of ingenuity, flexibility and astuteness to manoeuvre through the complex and almost impossible challenges facing him? He tried to conduct the war as best he could, sending out a myriad of orders and memoranda. Despite his reputation for competent command during the War of Independence, he was not able to see the big picture and give decisive command and control to the sprawling network of IRA divisions, a very difficult task. This is sharply illustrated by his failure to comprehend in early 1923 that the war was lost. In his frustration, he grasped at the straw of securing mountain artillery. There would be hit-and-run attacks on pro-Treaty forces, emerging from mountain fastnesses, using light, dismountable artillery pieces. Ironically it was on a bare mountain that Liam Lynch was mortally wounded.

Many people nowadays harbour the idea that the designation 'Republican' refers to the ending of partition. However, this concept featured little during the Civil War. The Unionists had proven that rigid intransigence worked with their metropolitan kith and kin. The northern entity (bearing the inaccurate title of Northern Ireland), with its parliament established in 1921, was a *fait accompli* by the time of the Treaty negotiations. The sop of the Boundary Commission (with implied transfer of large chunks of the six counties to the 26) was included in the Treaty. Pogroms erupted in the newly-hatched northern entity and Collins devised the subterfuge of attacks there, to kill it at birth, with a bonus of creating unity between the anti- and pro-Treaty sides. In reality Collins would not have been able to prise the British grip from the North, either covertly or overtly. The British would not have allowed it and would have flooded that part of Ireland with as many troops as were needed. However, if the Civil War had not occurred would Collins, Mulcahy and others have had the strength of will and negotiating skills to ensure that the Boundary Commission would work in the manner in which Lloyd George had so airily implied it would? As it turned out, the six counties were to continue as a sectarian backwater, with the nationalist minority abandoned to discriminatory Unionist rule (with no moderating British supervision) for much of the twentieth century.

Once the Civil War was won, the British left the Free State to its own devices. There was high unemployment, empty coffers and a damaged physical infrastructure. Even more seriously, there was a damaged moral infrastructure due to the ruthlessness in securing the State, which left a lasting legacy of bitterness. However, as de Valera discovered when he took power in 1932, the Free State had a surprising amount of independence.

The principal differences the protagonists fought over have long evaporated: we now have a 'Republic'; we are not members of the British Commonwealth (the present-day association of countries within the former Empire) and the oath to the monarch is long gone. Interestingly, what they really didn't fight about still has not been resolved: the partition of Ireland.

As the centenary approaches, it is to be hoped that there will be a better appreciation of what happened. A re-shaping of the major political parties into their ideological orientations, as opposed to their artificial Civil War origins, would be a significant advance. We should take note of what happened; let any lingering bitterness fall away; and, it is my earnest hope, propel our State, our island, towards a more cohesive and just one.

Michael B. Barry: Dublin, April 2014.

Chapter 1

The Growing Divide

The Irish War of Independence came to an end with the truce of July 1921. In October 1921, a delegation travelled to London for treaty talks which concluded when the Anglo-Irish Treaty was signed on 6 December. The Dáil debates that followed were punctuated by bitter uproar. The IRA was mainly anti-Treaty. Under the Treaty provisions a Provisional Government was established and a new army was formed. During the takeover of barracks, as British troops left, there was friction between both sides. Recruitment to the new army was stepped up. The IRA met to form an Executive which rejected the authority of the new government and it took over the Four Courts and other prominent buildings in Dublin in April 1922. In an effort to promote unity an election pact was made. The election was held on 16 June 1922 with a resulting majority for those with pro-Treaty views.

The truce came into effect on 11 July 1921. For the IRA, it offered a breathing space at a time when they were hard pressed. The painter, Leo Whelan, working from individual portraits, prepared this composite painting of the IRA GHQ Staff. At the time, the nationalist movement was a coalition of different groups with different aims and this painting captures some of the protagonists, who were to disagree and split in 1922. These include: (seated, from left), Michael Collins, Intelligence, and Richard Mulcahy, Chief of Staff, who later strongly supported the Treaty. Those who took a vastly divergent view include: (seated, fifth from left) Rory O'Connor, Director of Engineering, and Liam Mellows, Director of Purchases (standing, fourth from left).

Left: after the signing of the truce, de Valera led a delegation to London in mid-July 1921. Depicted here in a rather inaccurate portrait, he met the British PM, David Lloyd George. The outlines of the eventual Dominion-type settlement were presented by Lloyd George to de Valera but there was no meeting of minds. Later correspondence settled on a bland formula to allow negotiations to begin in October.

Right: some members of the Irish delegation, on the mailboat at Holyhead. en route to London for the October conference. De Valera had decided not to attend and later explained that this was in order to better prepare people for compromise.

Below: the might of the British Empire faces Ireland at the conference which began on 11 October 1921. Lloyd George, is in the centre on the left. On the right, the Irish delegation: (front to back), George Gavan Duffy, Robert Barton, Michael Collins, Arthur Griffith and Eamonn Duggan. Standing, Erskine Childers (principal secretary to the delegation).

Left: the Irish delegation at Hans Place. The odds were stacked against them: with unclear terms of reference, they were not united and some members like Childers reported directly back to de Valera. Lloyd George identified the main movers and had one-to-one meetings with Collins and Griffith. The latter was not in the same league as Lloyd George, a master of manipulation. The negotiations crashed against the rock of British intransigence, on the issues of allegiance to the King and membership of the British Empire, fundamental to the imperial mindset. Under pressure from Lloyd George's histrionics to sign or face renewed war, the delegation did not consult with Dublin and signed the Treaty in London on 6 December.

Left: the body language shows it all between the two gaunt men in the middle, here at a review in Co. Galway: the taller is Eamon de Valera, the other is Richard Mulcahy, Chief of Staff of the IRA. De Valera toured the west at the end of 1921 while the negotiations were ongoing in London. He emerged as the political leader of the anti-Treaty group; Mulcahy was to build up the new army of the Provisional Government and then resolutely lead it to victory in the Civil War.

Right: what the conflict was all about: the Anglo-Irish Treaty sets out, in 18 succinct paragraphs, how an Irish Free State would be formed, as a self-governing Dominion within "the Community of Nations known as the British Empire". It included: defence by sea was to be undertaken by the British, who would also retain naval ports; members of the Free State Parliament were to take an oath of allegiance to the constitution of the Irish Free State and to be "faithful to HM King George V"; the right of the Northern Ireland Parliament to opt out of the Irish Free State (which, to no one's surprise, it promptly did) and the sop of a Boundary Commission to be set up, if Northern Ireland did withdraw.

Heated debates in the Dáil followed and a vote on 7 January 1922 approved the Treaty by a narrow margin (64 to 57). Right: de Valera and his supporters on 10 January. He had declared the resignation of his cabinet and presidency the preceding day. A motion to re-elect him was narrowly defeated. On 14 January, the 'Southern Ireland Parliament' met in Dublin's Mansion House and elected a Provisional Government, in the absence of anti-Treaty members of the Dáil.

in Southern Ireland since the passing of the Government of Ireland Act, 1920, and for constituting a provisional Government, and the British Government shall take the steps necessary to transfer to such provisional Government the powers and machinery requisite for the discharge of its duties, provided that every member of such provisional Government shall have signified in writing his or her acceptance of this instrument. But this arrangement shall not continue in force beyond the expiration of twelve months from the date hereof.

18. This instrument shall be submitted forthwith by His Majesty's Government for the approval of Parliament and by the Irish signatories to a meeting summoned for the purpose of the members elected to sit in the House of Commons of Southern Ireland, and if approved shall be ratified by the necessary legislation.

On behalf of the Irish Delegation

On behalf of the British Delegation

December 6, 1921.

7.

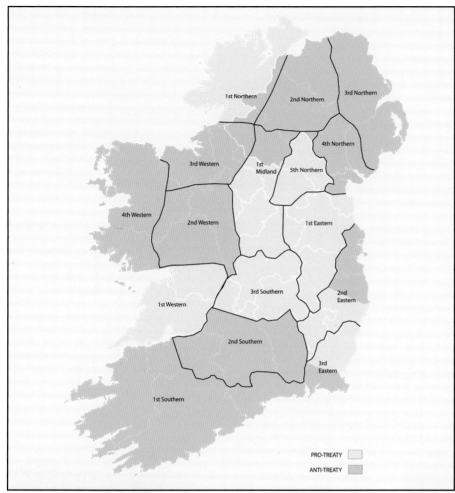

Left: how the IRA split. The response to the Treaty varied widely, in this army which was a federation of independent units. Often, it depended on the attitude of the local leader. In general, the areas that had been more active during the War of Independence were more strongly anti-Treaty.

Giving up the Republic declared in 1916 and asserted by the 1918 Dáil, for a lesser form of independence, was the main objection to the Treaty. An Irish Republic had been the shining goal in the struggle for independence since the time of Wolfe Tone. But apart from leaders like Liam Mellows and Peadar O'Donnell, there had been little analysis of what a republic would mean in reality.

Left: members of the anti-Treaty IRA patrol Dublin's Grafton Street. As the split crystallised, there was an understandable reluctance among the former comrades of the IRA to fight each other. The result was a plethora of meetings, truces and peace formulas. Amidst this confusion, the anti-Treaty IRA, then much stronger in numbers, did not capitalise on the many opportunities to seize power during these early days. In the meantime, the Provisional Government began to recruit its new army.

Above: the two principal protagonists of Northern Unionism, James Craig and Edward Carson.

The question of the partition of Ireland was not centre stage. Collins hoped to use a covert campaign against the six-county state as a unifying factor with the anti-Treaty forces. Nevertheless, the Northern Ireland Government, with British support and underpinned by a huge force of B Specials, was becoming an established fact. By the end of the Civil War, it was too late to impose any form of unity. Craig's sketch (right) in the Illustrated London News in April 1922 shows his understanding of the 'boundary question':
The three counties given up by Ulster in 1920: ≡
The portion now claimed by the South in 1922: |||

Right: Catholic refugees from northern pogroms flocked to Dublin. The IRA took over the Kildare Street Club to house them. Bridie Gallagher, a refugee, stands outside the club.

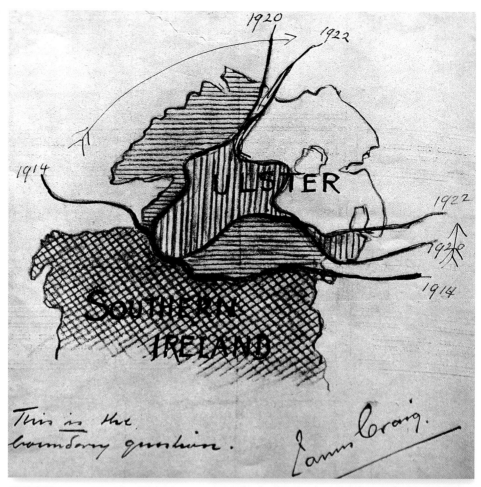

THE GUARDS BEGGARS BUSH IRISH REPUBLICAN ARMY
- THE MEN WHO FOUGHT FOR THE FREEDOM OF IRELP
(THE FIRST UNIT OF I.R.A. IN UNIFORM.)

The new army of the Provisional (later Free State) Government took over Beggar's Bush Barracks, in Dublin, from departing British troops on 31 January 1922 and set up headquarters there. In the following months, local forces, (either pro- or anti-Treaty, depending on the locality) occupied barracks as they were evacuated. Above: on 4 February the Dublin Guards line up at Beggars Bush with Commandant Paddy O'Daly, (by the drum). Lieutenant Padraig O'Connor stands to his right.

Left: Michael Collins arriving by taxi for the handover of Dublin Castle on 16 January 1922.

PANOGRAPH PHOTO CO
OF NEW YORK.
75 UPPER LEESON ST.
DUBLIN.

RY- 4TH 1922-.

Right: recruitment under-way for the Provisional Government army at Great Brunswick (Pearse) Street.
The anti-Treaty IRA flexed their muscles in their local territory during the first half of 1922. In the meantime, the Provisional Government rapidly built up its army. Outnumbered by the anti-Treaty IRA at the beginning of the Civil War (one estimate for these was around 13,000 men), the army rapidly grew in size. By July 1922 an establishment of 35,000 was authorised. At its peak in mid-1923, the army of the Free State amounted to around 55,000.

19

The IRA held a convention on 26 March 1922 where it re-affirmed its allegiance to the Republic and elected a 16-man Executive.
Left: Oscar Traynor, O/C Dublin Brigade, speaks at a parade of over 3,000 men at Smithfield, on 2 April 1922, to express support for the anti-Treaty IRA Executive. Rory O'Connor is on the left. Eleven days later he was one of the leaders of the occupation of the Four Courts.
Below: the First Southern Division (front row, fourth and fifth from left: Liam Lynch; Liam Deasy) at the second IRA Army Convention, in the Mansion House, on 9 April. The meeting ratified a new Republican Constitution.

Right: following what they regarded as misleading reports on the Army Convention, the anti-Treaty IRA destroyed the presses of the 'Freeman's Journal' at the end of March 1922.

Below right: the 'Freeman's Journal' was re-launched following the destruction of its presses. In its edition of 22 April 1922, it included this Shemus cartoon which depicts a Phoenix rising from the ashes of the wrecked plant. It holds a copy of the newspaper in its beak.

Below: daring piracy. The British auxillary armament ship 'Upnor', was captured by the IRA, about 50 km off the Irish coast, on 29 March 1922, en route from Haulbowline to Devonport, for delivery of (now) surplus armaments to Woolwich Arsenal. Hundreds of cases of rifles and machine guns, along with ammunition, were offloaded at Ballycotton, Co. Cork. This was a significant addition to the Republican armoury in the region.

Above: the strong, granite neo-classical walls of the Four Courts. The IRA Executive ordered that certain strategic buildings in Dublin be occupied. Among these was the Four Courts which was taken over as their headquarters on the night of 13 April.

Left: sandbags and rifles. IRA men on the roof of the Four Courts. After the occupation, the complex was progressively fortified; law books and ledgers were stuffed into windows.

Right: Rolls Royce armoured car at the Four Courts. In April 1922 it was captured by the anti-Treaty IRA at Templemore Barracks. Two weeks later, it was brought by Ernie O'Malley to the Four Courts. Christened 'The Mutineer', it was used during the June fighting. Later, on re-capture by the pro-Treaty forces, it was re-named 'The Ex-Mutineer' and saw action in Kerry after the Fenit landing in August 1922.

23

Left: Arthur Griffith arriving at Longford, en route to Sligo for a public meeting on Easter Sunday, 16 April 1922. Liam Pilkington, in charge of the Third Western Division, had proclaimed the meeting and the anti-Treaty IRA took over public buildings in the town. In response Comdt-General Seán Mac Eoin led his Provisional Government troops from Athlone, even wielding an axe himself to cut through felled trees that were blocking the road to the town.

Right: a watchful Seán MacEoin, Webley at the ready, overlooks the meeting in Sligo on Easter Sunday, from the first-floor window of a hotel.

Left: pro-Treaty men occupying Sligo Courthouse. With the area flooded by troops, the IRA desisted from interfering with Griffith's meeting.

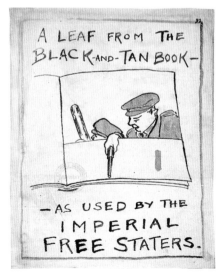

Left: vituperation on both sides. On the left, the proprietor of the 'Sligo Champion' calls the Republicans, who damaged his press to prevent him printing a report of Griffith's Easter meeting, the worst soubriquet of the time, the "Black and Tans". On the right, The same name is levelled at the Free State forces by Constance Markievicz, in one of her later series of cyclostyled propaganda handbills.

Left: Wellington Barracks (now Griffith College) was handed over to the Provisonal Government troops on 12 April 1922. Some days later there was a brief attack on the barracks by the anti-Treaty IRA. A heavier attack followed at the gates on 20 April. This lasted over an hour and involved an exchange of rifle fire and grenades. Five were wounded. Later, on 8 November 1922, the barracks came under sustained attack, as Republicans with rifles and machine guns opened up on a morning parade in the main square. A soldier and a civilian were killed and 17 soldiers wounded. In the aftermath a fleeing and wounded Republican was seized by troops from a house at nearby Donore Road and shot dead.

Left: 'La Tribuna Illustrata', in the deft style of their master illustrator, A. Minardi, depicts the 20 April attack on the "Caserma Wellington" by the "estremisti repubblicani" as a huge battle.

Right: some of the weapons of the Civil War.

1. Webley .455 service revolver. 2. Mauser 'Broomhandle' semi-automatic pistol. (popularly known as 'Peter the Painter')

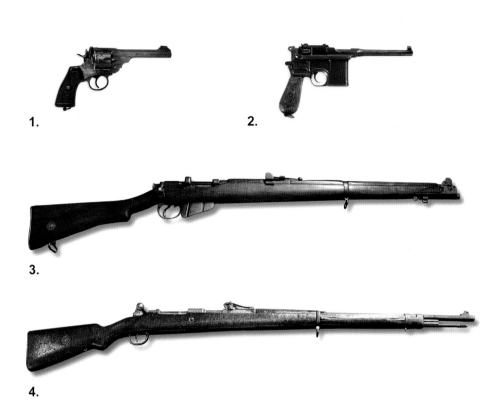

1.

2.

3. Short Magazine Lee Enfield Mk III. Standard issue, pro-Treaty army, also widely used by the IRA. Its efficient bolt action meant that a soldier could maintain a rapid rate of fire of its .303 bullets.

3.

4. Mauser Gewehr 98. With a five-round internal magazine of 7.92 mm calibre, this was the main rifle used by German infantry in WW I. Some were in use on the anti-Treaty side.

4.

5. It was in the Irish Civil War that the Thompson sub-machine gun, was first used in warfare. The drum magazines contained 50 or 100 bullets of .45 calibre. Several had been obtained by the IRA in 1921. (The first test was conducted by Tom Barry). A number were available to some IRA units during the war. The Thompson, portable and capable of deadly use in close encounters, acquired a menacing allure.

5.

6. Lancia armoured personnel carriers were adapted for the pro-Treaty army to operate on rail. This camouflaged version, which operated around Mallow, was known as the 'Grey Ghost'.

6.

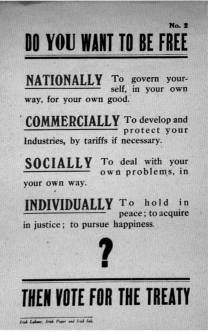

Near left: in this poster the Irish labour movement advocates a vote for the Treaty.

Far left: the Communist Party of Ireland was vigorously anti-Treaty as shown in this manifesto, that says "It is not a Free State: it is a Slave State". Unusually for a communist party, the text invokes a deity: "Oh God! to think that the people of Ireland are asked to renounce the Republic..."

Workers, dissatisfied with their conditions, from the Limerick Soviet of 1919 onwards, occupied their places of work. In 1922 this included the chain of Cleeves dairy works across the south. With a few exceptions, there was little sympathy for workers' rights from the anti-Treaty IRA and definitely none from the pro-Treaty side. These actions, against the background of events in Bolshevik Russia, made bourgeois Ireland nervous of a communist takeover as a result of the disorder of the Civil War.

Left: a Shemus cartoon in the 'Freeman's Journal' of 2 August 1922, shows Trotsky saying to the ailing Lenin: "Cheer up Comrade Lenin: I've just learned, Ireland is ours for the taking!" Lenin – very sick: "I seem to have heard that before!"

With elections planned for 16 June 1922, both sides made a pact in May with an agreed list of candidates. Right: Eamon de Valera speaks at a rally at Mooncoin, Co. Kilkenny on 13 June. This fastidious and then-respected leader had taken a complex approach against the Treaty during the Dáil debates. On 17 March, he said in a speech at Thurles that if the Treaty were ratified, the Volunteers "would have to wade through Irish blood." Later, he said these speeches were to warn of civil war, rather than be an incitement to conflict. During the Civil War he kept a faint political flame burning but was sidelined by the IRA leadership.

Right: Michael Collins speaks in Cork in April 1922. Two days before the June election he spoke again in Cork. Cutting against the grain of the electoral pact, he urged the attendance to vote for the best candidates.

This election was not an example of perfect democracy: it was held in the ongoing shadow of the British threat of war if the Treaty was not accepted. The anti-Treaty side fared badly: only 36 of their candidates were elected, while 58 of the pro-Treaty side were successful. Labour and others (who generally supported the Treaty) gained 34 seats.

Above: Bristol F.2b Fighter at Hendon Museum near London. Since the beginning of 1922, the British forces in Ireland had been wound down; those remaining were mainly confined to barracks within an arc around Dublin. Left and below: the logbook of a Bristol Fighter (later to be BF No. I in the Irish Army Air Service) shows that, while in RAF service, it was carrying out escort duties for trains transporting British troops from Dublin to Belfast in April 1922.

Date.	Hour.	Pilot.	Passenger.	Route.	Time in Air.	
					hrs.	mins.
				Brought forward ...	134	30
22·3·22	16·25	S/L. Wyne Eyton	Mechanic	Aerodrome		20
23·3·22	14·15	F/O. Gemmel	Mechanic	Aerodrome		20
4·4·22	10·50	F/O. Gemmel	Mechanic	Local Formation		40
10·4·22	10·45	F/O. Fleming	F/O. Clark	Reconnaissance	1	15
11·4·22	10·45	S/L. Wyne Eyton	2AC Franks.	Engine Test		15
11·4·22	11·05	S/L. Wyne Eyton	2M. Bosworth	—		10
11·4·22	15·50	F/O. Dix Lewis	H. Hooper	Local		10
13·4·22	08·15	F/O. Dix Lewis	F/Sgt. Vather	Train Escort. Dundalk Dublin		25
" — "	10·15	F/O. Dix Lewis	F/Sgt. Vather	Train Escort.	1	55
" — "	12·50	F/O. Dix Lewis	F/Sgt. Vather	Train Escort	1	20
" — "	15·00	F/O. Dix Lewis	F/Sgt. Vather	Gormanstown - Baldonnel		25
				Carried forward	141	5

Chapter 2

Shell & Shot

There were many flare-ups between the opposing sides during the first half of 1922 which increased the likelihood of conflict. The assassination of Sir Henry Wilson in London and the kidnapping of a pro-Treaty general proved to be the final triggers for the Civil War. Bombardment of the Four Courts commenced on 28 June 1922. Days of shelling ended with the storming of the buildings. A massive explosion sent the contents of the Public Record Office into oblivion. The anti-Treaty IRA took over buildings in central Dublin including the so-called 'Block' on Upper Sackville Street. By 5 July the Block, in ruins, was cleared of resistance. As Republicans fled the city, the war moved to the rest of the country.

Longford-born Field Marshal Sir Henry Wilson had been Chief of the Imperial General Staff and was vociferous in his opposition to the Treaty. As security advisor to the newly created entity of Northern Ireland, which was riven by sectarian pogroms, he became a hate figure to all shades of nationalist opinion. Left: an eerily prescient Shemus cartoon in the 'Freeman's Journal' of 8 June 1922, reflects the general dislike for Wilson. Titled 'Henry the Ruthless', it depicts Wilson with his orderly, a skeletal grim reaper. The exchange runs: Orderly: "All is quiet in the salient, Sir!" Wilson: "But there's a hell of a row everywhere else."

Below left: plaque to Sir Henry Wilson at Liverpool Street Station in London. He had just unveiled an adjacent WW I memorial on 22 June 1922 here and was shot two hours later. He had been trailed back to his home by two London-based IRA volunteers. The British Cabinet met immediately, in a state of agitation. Lloyd George wrote to Michael Collins stating that the IRA were to blame; the continuing Four Courts occupation, as well as the ambiguous situation of the IRA, could no longer be tolerated. Right: the 'Petit Journal Illustré' depicts the assassination.

TO THE MEMORY OF
FIELD MARSHAL SIR HENRY WILSON BART
G.C.B. D.S.O. M.P
WHOSE DEATH OCCURRED ON THURSDAY 22ND JUNE 1922
WITHIN TWO HOURS OF HIS UNVEILING
THE ADJOINING MEMORIAL

ABONNEMENTS

Trois mois Six mois Un an
FRANCE & COLONIES
4 fr.   7 fr. 50 14 fr.
UNION POSTALE
6 fr.   12 fr.   22 fr.

Le Petit Journal
illustré

PARAISSANT LE DIMANCHE
33e Année - N° 1645
On s'abonne dans tous
les bureaux de poste
Les Manuscrits ne sont pas rendus

Un assassinat politique

L'histoire du conflit entre l'Irlande et la Grande-Bretagne a toutes ses pages tachées de sang. — Un nouveau chapitre dramatique vient d'y être ajouté. A Londres, le maréchal Wilson a été assassiné à coups de revolvers par deux fanatiques Irlandais. C'est un brave soldat et un ami de la France qui vient de disparaître.

After Wilson's assassination, the British planned to launch an attack on the Four Courts on 25 June 1922, but were dissuaded by the commander of British forces in Ireland, General Macready.

The next significant event occurred on 26 June. The anti-Treaty IRA raided Ferguson's motor garage, a branch of a Belfast firm, on Lower Baggot Street and commandeered cars, (considered as imported in defiance of the Belfast Boycott, then being organised by anti-Treaty forces). Pro-Treaty troops arrived and surrounded the premises, as seen here (left). The leader of the raiding party, Commandant Leo Henderson, director of the Belfast Boycott, was captured and transferred to Mountjoy Gaol.

In retaliation, Lieut-General JJ 'Ginger' O'Connell, Deputy Chief of Staff, (left) was kidnapped later that night, when, having left his fiancée's house, he walked alone, in uniform and unarmed, towards Beggar's Bush Barracks. O'Connell was brought to the Four Courts where he had to endure the subsequent bombardment. O'Connell was popular in the army and this abduction proved to be the final event which propelled the Provisional Government to begin the assault on the Four Courts.

Above: the gunners' view; this present-day vista of Gandon's Four Courts is similar to that presented to the newly-fledged gunners of the pro-Treaty army as dawn broke on 28 June 1922. The Dublin Guards, under Paddy O'Daly, had sealed off the surrounding area the previous evening. An ultimatum to evacuate the building was given to the occupants at 3:40 am. The first shells were fired from Winetavern Street shortly after 4 am. The Civil War had begun and the confusion of the previous six months crystallised into a simple proposition: a 'Free State' or 'Republic'. Right: an 18-pounder at the corner of Lower Bridge Street and Merchant's Quay, shielded by a Lancia armoured personnel carrier.

Above: shelling the Four Courts from Winetavern Street. Two 18-pounder guns are in operation, shielded by Lancias. The inexperience of the gunners is shown by the breaches on the southern quay walls. The bombardment is well under way as seen by the pockmarks on the Four Courts buildings opposite. A Lancia can be seen jammed against the right-hand gates, to prevent the exit of the anti-Treaty IRA's captured Rolls Royce armoured car.

Left: shells, ready and laid out in wood-shavings.

Right: map of the Four Courts area.

The pro-Treaty army received two 18-pounders from the British at Marlborough (now McKee) Barracks on the evening of 27 June. Two more field guns were obtained the following day. A memoir by a British Army Lance-Bombardier claims that, on a night, his unit set up their 60-pounder howitzers and fired two rounds at the Four Courts. However there is no corroborating evidence.

It was incongruous for what was essentially a guerilla army (and their leadership elite) to set up in a static, easily besieged position. Most of this leadership was captured when the Four Courts fell. However, the defenders of the Four Courts, for most of the siege, had some communications with the outside. They could send and receive a limited number of messages, usually conveyed by members of Cumann na mBan. Right: the initial communiqué from the Four Courts defenders, which exhibits a degree of self-confidence and optimism for the future. It was published in Poblacht na hÉireann, a broadsheet, which presented the war from the Republican viewpoint for the rest of 1922 and into 1923.

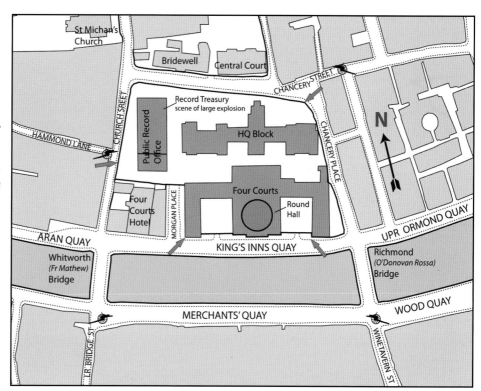

STOP PRESS

POBLACHT NA h-EIREANN

Wednesday, June 28th, Seventh Year of the Republic.

COMMUNIQUE FROM THE FOUR COURTS

We have received the following message from Major General Rory O'Connor, I.R.A.:

9 a.m., Wednesday, June 28th

At 3.40 a.m. this morning we received a note signed by Tom Ennis demanding on behalf of "The Government" our surrender at 4 a.m. when he would attack.

He opened attack at 4.07 in the name of his <u>Government</u>, with Rifle, Machine and field pieces.

THE BOYS ARE GLORIOUS, AND WILL FIGHT FOR THE REPUBLIC TO THE END. HOW LONG WILL OUR MISGUIDED FORMER COMRADES OUTSIDE ATTACK THOSE WHO STAND FOR IRELAND ALONE?

Three casualties so far, all slight. Father Albert and Father Dominic with us here.

Our love to all comrades outside, and the brave boys especially of the Dublin Brigade.

(Signed) RORY O'CONNOR,

Four Courts.   Major General, I.R.A.

The Republic is fighting for its life.
The Republic proclaimed in arms at Easter, 1916, established by law in January, 1919, defended by an army and people with heroic bravery and sacrifice through Terror, torture, and devastation in 1920 and 1921 : the Republic consecrated by the blood of Pearse, Connolly, and the dearest and noblest of our patriots : the Republic once more is fighting for its life.
Citizens, defend your Republic!
The enemy is the old enemy, England; using new weapons lent her, to their shame, by traitors to the Republic in our midst. Mr. Churchill cracked the whip in his speech on Monday night when he ordered the Provisional Government to attack the Four Courts. His Free State agents have obeyed. Shame on them Shane !
Mercenaries wearing Irish uniform, paid, equipped, and armed by England, and acting under England's orders, are attacking our brothers of the Irish Republican Army, who defend the living Republic, and will defend it to the death.
In the Four Courts, bombarded by guns borrowed from Churchill, and attacked by troops armed by Churchill, stand the men who have refused to forswear their allegiance to the Republic, who have refused to sacrifice honour for expediency, and sell their country to a foreign King. In Rory O'Connor and his comrades lives the onslaught, indomitable soul of Ireland.
Irish citizens, give them support! Irish soldiers, bring them aid!

Left: pro-Treaty snipers set up on the tower of St Michan's Church, Church Street, which overlooks the Four Courts.

Right: an Ordnance QF 18-pounder Field Gun Mk II. (In this version, the recuperator, which returns the gun after the recoil, to firing position, is below the barrel.) Mobile and quick-firing, the 18-pounder was the standard British field gun in WW I.

Below right: this record for Field Gun No. 10756 lists 375 shells fired at the Four Courts, as well as details of shells fired during subsequent actions in Drogheda and Cork. At an early stage, high-explosive shells ran short. The British had only shrapnel shells in stock (anti-personnel shells, which emitted hundreds of small balls, useless against the granite walls.) These were issued, as General Macready, wrote, "simply to make a noise through the night". A destroyer had been dispatched to an arsenal at Carrickfergus for the necessary shells. The resupply of high-explosive shells allowed the eventual creation of several large breaches in the walls around the Four Courts.

Left: shell, from the June 1922 fighting, recovered from the grounds of the Capuchin Friars in Church Street, a short distance from the Four Courts complex.

Record of Rounds Fired.

Ship or Station	Date	Proof Cordite				Full Cordite				¾ Cordite				½ Cordite				Blank	† Total number of equivalent full rounds	Remarks
		Powder	Nature			Powder	Nature			Powder	Nature			Powder	Nature					
			Mk.I.	MD	MDT	Size		Mk.I.	MD	MDT	Size		Mk.I.	MD	MDT	Size		Mk.I.	MD	MDT	Size			

Ship or Station	Date	Powder	Mk.I.	MD	MDT	Size	Powder	Mk.I.	MD	MDT	Size	Powder	Mk.I.	MD	MDT	Size	Powder	Mk.I.	MD	MDT	Size	Blank	Total	Remarks
Meanwood	24·7·18			3		8			1		8												7	For Evan. see Page 1
28/6/'22 and during Four County Operations	28·6·22								375.		8												375	John & Boyle Capt I.N. Army
Millmount Drogheda	4/7/22.								40		8												40	John & Boyle Capt
Passage West, Cork	8/8/22								25		8												25	John & Boyle Capt
									ROB		8													
GLEN IMAAL	1·9·25								·6		8												6	Brennan Lt 14...
" "	2·9·25								11		8												11	do
" "	4·9·25								7		8												7	do
" "	7·9·25								·5·		8												5	do —
" "	9·9·25								4		8												4	do
" "	11·9·25								10		8												10	do
KILDARE	1935																					16	1	do Brennan...
Total to																							491.	do...
Glen Imaal	21/4/26								6		8												6	do
do do	23/4/26								3		8												3.	do
do do	29/4/26								10		8												10.	do

39

Scenes during the Dublin fighting.

Above: a posed photograph of pro-Treaty troops, along with a supporter in civilian clothes. The defiant Republican Easter Week poster, was prescient, in an unintended way: in both the Four Courts and the 'Block', the anti-Treaty side had encamped in fixed (and possibly sacrificial) locations, allowing for easy siege by a well-armed army, just like 1916.

Left: pro-Treaty soldiers haul an 18-pounder into place.

Right: carved detail, appropriately with a cannon, at the Royal Hospital Kilmainham. As well as being a home for retired soldiers of the British Army, it was also the quarters of General Sir Nevil Macready, Commander-in-Chief of the British Army in Ireland. There was some surprise when a shrapnel shell exploded over the Royal Hospital grounds on the morning of 29 June. In this embarrassing episode it transpired that a gunner situated to the north-east of the Four Courts had canted up his 18-pounder (newly acquired from the British) at a sniper atop the dome. The shell passed through the dome and continued in a south-westerly direction towards the Royal Hospital. Maj-General Emmet Dalton had to apologise for the incident.

Right: after 3 pm, on 29 June, pro-Treaty troops stormed the Four Courts through newly-created gaps in the walls. One was at Morgan's Place, where the assault proved difficult. Another was here, at Church Street, where Commandant Padraig O'Connor led his troops through the breach. They captured some surprised defenders. O'Connor explored the Record Office and saw that it had been prepared for fire. Holes had been cut in floors, with blankets draped through.

On the morning of 30 June the headquarters block at the rear was on fire. Flames were reaching the Public Record Office on the western end. The fighting was at its height when at around 12:30 pm there was an enormous explosion in the Record Office. Many pro-Treaty troops were injured. Two more explosions took place in the Round Hall area at around 2 pm. The defenders surrendered at 3:45 pm.

Left: conflagration at the Four Courts. The massive explosion, the largest Dublin has ever experienced, results in clouds of black smoke and debris billowing high above the city.

Left: Grant of Probate of the will of Margaret Fitzmaurice, a document recovered after the explosion, being restored at the National Archives. The state-of-the-art and supposedly safe, Public Record Office had stored irreplaceable Irish medieval documents, maps, census, administrative and court records. Later in the Commons, on the day of the explosion, the ever-quotable Winston Churchill said: "A state without archives is better than archives without a state!" He wrote to Michael Collins afterwards: "The archives of the Four Courts may be scattered but the title-deeds of Ireland are safe."

The cause of the explosion, that resulted in the destruction of many of Ireland's most precious documents, has been disputed. There are several facts: the occupiers had set up a munitions factory in the basement of the Record Office and stored tonnes of explosives there; a letter (right) issued on 29 June by Oscar Traynor O/C Dublin Brigade IRA (who took over part of Sackville Street that day), refers to a request to the Four Courts garrison to blow their mines "as a signal of their retirement"; shelling of the Four Courts continued on 30 June; Brig-General O'Daly declared to the press, immediately after the surrender, that the huge explosion was caused by a mine which they were planning to disarm. However, it has never been resolved whether the large explosion that occurred against the confused maelstrom of shelling, bullets, fire and smoke in the huge Four Courts complex, packed as it was with mines and explosives, was caused intentionally or accidentally.

Right: passers-by on Sackville Street pick up documents from the Public Record Office. Later, the Government set up an office in the Royal Society of Antiquaries of Ireland at Merrion Square to receive any salvaged documents.

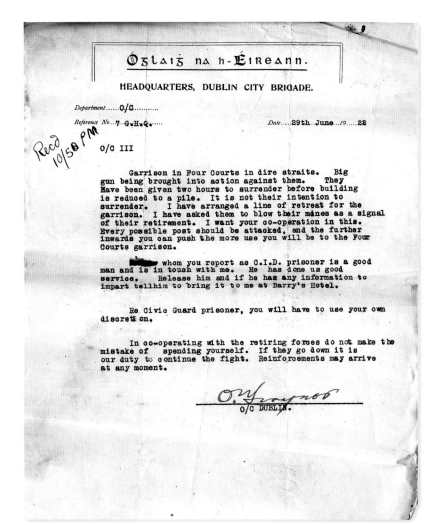

Left: after the battle for the Four Courts, the building lay in total ruin. In the Round Hall, once described as the "physical and spiritual centre of the building", the dome had collapsed, following the explosions that occurred there in mid-afternoon on 30 June. Edward Smyth (the eighteenth-century sculptor whose work adorns many of the prominent Georgian buildings in Dublin) had extensively decorated the interior, most of which was destroyed during the hostilities. There had been a series of plaster statues depicting Dublin legal luminaries, which were placed in front of the alcoves around the hall. This is the damaged statue of Henry Joy, Chief Baron of the Irish Exchequer, (a cousin of the United Irishman leader, Henry Joy McCracken) whose battered form casts a ghostly pall over the rubble.

Left: looking down from the dome, a present-day view of the Round Hall of the Four Courts. The statues which had been located in front of the alcoves were not replaced during the reconstruction of the 1920s.

During their occupation of the Four Courts, the Republicans had commandeered a large collection of vehicles, including around a dozen cars taken during the raid on Ferguson's garage at Baggot Street. (These cars had been intended for an expedition to the North, led by Peadar O'Donnell). The vehicles had been stored in the grounds of the Four Courts. Right: in the aftermath, a car lies submerged under rubble amidst the devastation.

In the background is the ruined Record Treasury section of the Public Record Office, with its tall windows and now missing its glass roof, due to the huge explosion that had occurred here on 30 June. Ironically, to specially protect its precious contents, the Record Treasury had been built with sealed iron doors. There was also an isolation space between it and the adjacent but separate Record House.

Right: these two Capuchin priests were in the Four Courts during the siege. As well as giving spiritual comfort and helping with evacuating the wounded, they acted as intermediaries in negotiating surrender by the Republican occupiers. From left, Fr Albert Bibby and Fr Dominic O'Connor.

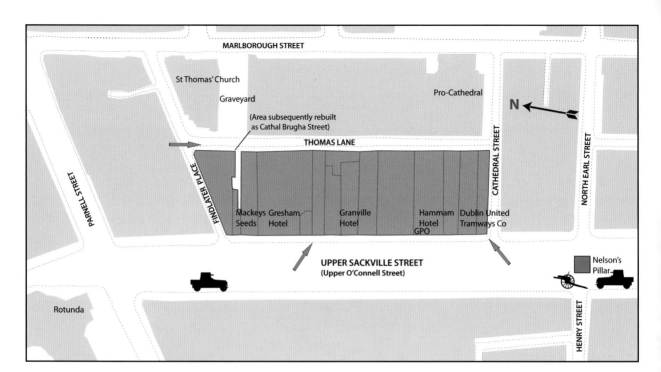

Above: map of the 'Block' area. As the siege of the Four Courts entered its final stage on 29 June, the IRA took over buildings around central Dublin to relieve the pressure. This included what became known as the 'Block' on Sackville (now O'Connell) Street. With a frontage of around 200 metres, it ranged from Findlater Place to Cathedral Street and included the Gresham, Granville, & Hammam Hotels. It was not an ideal location, being on the east side of Upper Sackville Street, and thus isolated from the Four Courts garrison. Oscar Traynor, O/C, set up his headquarters in the Hammam Hotel.

Left: present-day view of the reconstructed buildings on Upper O'Connell Street.

By the end of 2 July, outlying areas had been cleared and pro-Treaty forces now surrounded the Block. As the attack intensified, the main IRA force withdrew on 3 July, leaving a small group under Cathal Brugha. Eventually, on the evening of 4 July, an 18-pounder (above, protected by two Lancia armoured personnel carriers) was set up at the corner of Henry Street to shell the Block.

Right: Provisional Government troops fire their Lee Enfields during the Dublin fighting; ejected cartridge cases lie around them.

Above: with Nelson's Pillar in the background, pro-Treaty troops fire at the Block from the top of Henry Street.

Left: at Henry Street, an armoured Lancia personnel carrier is parked to shield the troops from sniper fire. The chalked slogan refers to the nickname 'Trucers.' This reflected the pro-Treaty perception that many flocked to join the anti-Treaty IRA after the truce in 1921, having played no part in the War of Independence. The other side harboured a similar opinion about their pro-Treaty opponents.

Right: armoured cars played a major part in the fighting around Sackville Street. Here, on Henry Street, is a Rolls Royce armoured car. It has been named 'Customs House', presumably in memory of the IRA action during the War of Independence which destroyed that building. Bitterness at the beginning of the Civil War is evident from the figure of 'Rory Boy' with a noose around its neck. Rory O' Connor had just been captured after the surrender of the Four Courts. Fourteen of these armoured cars, dubbed 'Whippets', were acquired from the British. These formidable armoured vehicles were over five metres long and weighed over four tonnes. Clearly seen are the protective shutters over the radiator at the front, closed here, during the fighting.

Right: this Provisional Government soldier, rifle at the ready, warily investigates the next room, beyond the hole in the wall in a building opposite the Hammam Hotel. In the close-quarters fighting, walls had been punched through to get from one building to another. This tactic ('mouseholing' as it was called at the time) was used by both sides, particularly by the anti-Treaty forces who opened corridors along the whole Block.

Left: Provisional Government soldiers seek an advantageous position. Such urban fighting is one of the most difficult forms of combat. Here we see soldiers inside the Royal Bank of Ireland premises on Sackville Street.

Left: over the duration of the Civil War, relatively few photographs were taken of Republican fighters – understandable, given the practicalities of their guerrilla fighting. By contrast, on the Government side, facilitated by its efficient propaganda department, many photographs were posed for the press, like this one staged for the camera during the fighting around Sackville Street. The symmetry and composition of these two soldiers, posing, in wht looks like a yard, on a timber frame with their Lee Enfield Mk III rifles, is excellent.

Above: on O'Connell Street today – the Hammam Buildings.

Right: on Upper Sackville Street, a Lancia armoured personnel carrier and a Rolls Royce armoured car, of the Provisional Government army, manoeuvre along by the Hammam Hotel and adjacent buildings of the Block. The façade is badly damaged by bullets and shell-fire. A soldier, clutching his rifle, clambers out from the back of the armoured car.

Right: ready for ignition. In front of the Mackey's Seeds premises and guarded by two watchful comrades standing by containers of petrol, a Provisional Government officer fires through a window of the adjacent Gresham Hotel. The intention is to place incendiaries and flush out the opposing forces within.

CATHAL BRUGHA
1874 — 1922

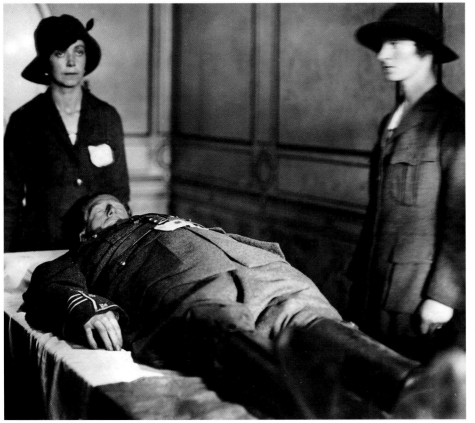

Left: memorial plaque to Cathal Brugha, at the southern end of the former Block at the corner of O'Connell Street and Cathedral Street. It is located high on a wall, incongruously situated above a fast food restaurant.

Cathal Brugha was one of the foremost protagonists on the anti-Treaty side. He was principled, prickly and determined. He had demonstrated his bravery during the 1916 Rising. As the pro-Treaty forces gained the upper hand in the fighting at the Block, most of the Republican defenders had managed to escape. On 5 July, Brugha was in charge of a small rearguard group, having retreated to the Granville Hotel. At around 7 pm, with the hotel in flames, Brugha ordered his men to surrender. Then he emerged into Thomas' Lane, behind the hotel, pistol in hand, and ran towards a party of troops. Shots rang out and he was hit by a single bullet. Wounded in a femoral artery, he died two days later.

Left. Cathal Brugha laid out in the mortuary of the Mater Hospital, flanked by a Cumann na mBan guard of honour. One account relates, poignantly, that the only volunteer uniform that was available was a little large for Brugha, a small man.

Right: in a photograph taken from a building opposite the Block on Upper Sackville Street, another view of the devastation. Two Lancias are parked on the street outside the Hammam Hotel, with a gaping hole in the entrance caused by 18-pounder shells. By nightfall on 5 July, the Hammam Hotel, pounded by shells and then set abaze, had been razed to the ground.

Right: a feature of the battles in Dublin in 1916 and again in July 1922 was that they attracted a large number of onlookers. Since the lure of the spectacle obviously outweighed the real danger from stray bullets, a large crowd assembles at the south end of O'Connell Bridge to observe the destruction at the upper end of Sackville Street, beyond Nelson's Pillar. General Macready harrumphed in his memoirs that, during the fighting in the city, Dubliners lined up with interest and amusement and were kept in place by policemen "in the same way as at a festival or a Lord Mayor's show".

Left: when the fighting ended on 5 July, 1922, the Block was in ruins having succumbed to bullets, shells and flames. Some buildings had totally collapsed. Others, like the Gresham Hotel here, stood with little more than a ravaged façade, a few cross walls and a forlorn cast-iron portico.

In the meantime the Republican fighters had escaped from the city. The next phase of the war was about to begin with the fighting mainly concentrated outside of Dublin.

Left: 'Dublin Opinion' portrays a soldier in central Dublin. "Arrived alright. Am staying at Gresham."

Left: enemies all around. Provisional Government soldiers, bristling with weapons, pose for the camera against the backdrop of the ruined Four Courts.

Above: the devastation of the Block on Upper Sackville Street after the fighting, as seen from the top of Nelson's Pillar. This was the second destruction on the street, just over six years after that of the 1916 Easter Rising.

Right: a temporary GPO (note the new 'An Post' branding) had been set up on Upper Sackville Street, while the GPO was being rebuilt after the destruction of 1916. This post office (part of what became the Block) was also devastated in the fighting of July 1922.

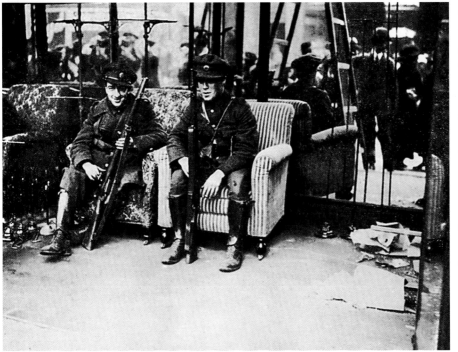

Above: men, attributed as anti-Treaty, emerge under guard, from the Edinburgh Life Assurance building on the west side of Upper Sackville Street. Is this at an early stage of the fighting? The well-attired group stride out with confidence and vigour.

Left: although the pro-Treaty army was newly formed, some of its men could behave like the proverbial 'old soldier'. Spotting the opportunity, they take a break in the armchairs of a store. They are guarding against looting on Henry Street.

Above: in Dublin, carts, trams and vans. The hunt is on for anti-Treaty men and arms.

Right: near O'Connell Bridge, prisoners are loaded into this Lancia armoured personnel carrier, as a paper-seller looks on. In contrast to those emerging from the Edinburgh Life Assurance building (top, opposite), this is a scene towards the end of the Dublin fighting. Some prisoners are bloodied, all look exhausted and apprehensive.

Above: permanent way men repair the track of the Dublin & Blessington Steam Tramway, damaged by the IRA. The South Dublin Brigade, IRA, destroyed Rathfarnham police station on 30 June and travelled to meet up with other Republicans assembling at Blessington, where the original plan was to march on Dublin.

Left: soldiers at Crooksling, on the road to Blessington, on 5 July. When large numbers of Provisional Government troops converged on Blessington, there was little resistance and they found the Republicans had dispersed.

Chapter 3
War in the Country

As the main conflict moved out of Dublin, there were clashes between pro- and anti-Treaty forces across the country. Limerick, on the Shannon was a strategic point between Munster and Connaught. In a re-run of the Dublin conflict, the Provisional Government army took the city from the anti-Treaty IRA and the fighting moved to the nearby Kilmallock region. After large-scale encounters the pro-Treaty side prevailed. With the help of an artillery piece, Waterford was easily captured from the Republicans. As towns were taken along the River Suir, the anti-Treaty 'Munster Republic' was being reduced. There was shock on both sides after the prominent Republican Harry Boland was mortally wounded in Skerries.

Left: in July 1922 Liam Lynch was Chief of Staff of the anti-Treaty IRA. Born in 1893, he came from a farm near Mitchelstown. He had established a reputation as an able military leader in the south during the War of Independence and was a senior member of the IRB. Honourable and lacking in guile, he made strenuous efforts to find common ground with the opposing side during the first half of 1922. However, once the bombardment of the Four Courts began, he headed south to direct resistance to the Treaty. En route, he was briefly detained by pro-Treaty troops, but released. There was the mistaken assumption that Lynch, who was held in high regard, would be neutral in the conflict. Back in Cork on 29 June, he issued an order to the IRA whereby he hoped "to have made rapid progress towards complete control of west and southern Ireland for the Republic". The next day Lynch went to Limerick and set up his HQ in the New Barracks there. He was conscious of the importance of the Limerick-Waterford line, which delineated the so-called 'Munster Republic' where the anti-Treaty forces held complete sway. Lynch moved his HQ to Clonmel on 11 July and later to Fermoy.

Right: King John's Castle in Limerick. The city, astride the river Shannon, controlled approaches to the south-west and the north-west. There had been maneouverings here between the two sides in March. One of the few pro-Treaty leaders of the IRA, Comdt-General Michael Brennan, commander of the First Western Division realised this, saying "The whole Civil War turned on Limerick". He moved his soldiers from East Clare to the city. Republican forces were entrenched in the majority of Limerick's many barracks and other strongholds – and more were converging there. Brennan and his colleague, Donncadh O'Hannigan, with few soldiers and rifles at their disposal, entered in to negotiations and signed a truce on 4 July with Liam Lynch. This bought time for the pro-Treaty side. Troops and arms were now sent to Brennan in Limerick by circuitous routes. The truce ended on 11 July, when the Provisional Government forces, on the pretext that a soldier had been shot, spread out along the barricaded streets of the city and opened fire on the Ordnance Barracks.

Right: anti-Treaty forces park their commandeered cars in front of the Imperial Hotel in Limerick.

Above: this magnificent panorama by Frank Imbusch captures the scene of barricades and barbed wire on O'Connell Street and surroundings, under Republican control.

Fierce fighting continued and both sides received reinforcements. In the days that followed, Provisional Government troops attacked anti-Treaty positions, using armoured cars and machine guns. On occasion, a home-made armoured car of the Cork IRA entered the fray.

Left: pro-Treaty soldiers pose for the camera at King John's Castle at Limerick.

As fighting continued in Limerick, General Eoin O'Duffy, newly-appointed GOC South-Western Command, left Dublin with troops, weapons, armoured car and an 18-pounder. He reached Killaloe and fought his way into Limerick on 19 July.

Right: in a jovial mood. The senior command in the city: O'Duffy on left; in centre, cigarette in hand, Comdt-General Michael Brennan; next right, Comdt-General Fionán Lynch, TD; extreme right, just in view, Comdt-General WRE Murphy, (formerly a Lieut-Colonel in the South Staffordshire Regiment.)

Above: after shelling in the city, Republicans withdrew from the New Barracks and set it on fire. Looting by civilians can be seen in this Imbusch panorama.

The arrival of the 18-pounder made all the difference. The gun was placed directly across the river from Strand Barracks (left, present-day view). On 20 July shelling opened breaches in the walls, allowing the storming of the barracks. Next, Castle Barracks was shelled. In face of the onslaught, Liam Lynch sent an order to the anti-Treaty forces to abandon their now-untenable positions and burn them.

Right: Strand Barracks after capture.

Above: Imbusch portrays the starkness of the New Barracks, totally burnt out.

Left: At Limerick railway sheds, well-armed pro-Treaty supporters, including a uniformed soldier, pose in front of armoured wagons.

Right: no shortage of weapons – and glad to have them. Pro-Treaty forces at Limerick assemble during the July events.

sᵹéᴀl
ᴄᴀᴛᴀ luimniᵹe

PRICE 1d   (LIMERICK WAR NEWS)

VOL. I   FRIDAY, 11th AUGUST, 1922   NO. XXVI

The Irish Commander-in-Chief

The Man who broke the Black and Tan Terror.

General Michael Collins, C. in C., Irish Army

IRELAND'S HERO

General Collins is Commander-in-Chief of the Irish Army.

He is the man who fought the Black and Tan Terror.

He is now fighting the native terrorist.

The Black and tans were beaten.

The mutineers are also being crushed.

If they were not, the expulsion of the alien forces who held the country in slavery for centuries, would have been in vain.

General Collins realises this. He has set himself to the task.

He shall not fail to accomplish it.

Answer His Call.

Above: looking war-weary, Provisional Government troops take a break outside the Household Bazaar Company premises, William Street, Limerick.

Republicans withdrew from the city and regrouped in the Kilmallock-Bruree area, close to the border with anti-Treaty Cork. After consolidating his hold on Limerick, in the last week of July, O'Duffy sent Comdt-General WRE Murphy and his troops to the area.

Left: in the period following the fighting in the Limerick region, the Provisional Government army produced this propaganda sheet 'Limerick War News'.

Right: in parallel with the final thrust against Kilmallock, Adare to the south-west of Limerick was also attacked. As they advanced on 4 August, the pro-Treaty forces came under fire from a machine gun situated on top of this tower at the Church of Ireland church at the entrance to the town. An 18-pounder was set up, on the opposite side of the River Maigue, and fired shells in reply. The troops took Adare that evening.

Right: Provisional Government soldiers escort a prisoner at the 'South-Western Front', as the press called the fighting zone in the Limerick region. In the early part of the Civil War, relations between both sides were relatively relaxed, and bitterness was not widespread. All was to change over the months that followed. Here, the soldier to the left grins to the camera while the young IRA volunteer looks a little abashed.

Left: a multi-arch masonry bridge over a tributary of the River Maigue. It was blown up by Republicans hurriedly retreating to Bruree, as the Provisional Government army advanced under the command of Comdt-General WRE Murphy. The bridge was partially demolished. The arches were short span, thus easily filled with rubble to allow passage of the commandeered truck from Limerick hauling the 18-pounder. Fighting was fierce on a wide front. The Provisional Government forces moved to encircle Kilmallock in a great arc to the north of the town. An attack, using artillery, began on 4 August. There was limited resistence to the advance but no great final battle. The town was taken taken at 5 am the following morning. Most of the defenders had withdrawn. The Kerry IRA Brigades also had evacuated to face the pro-Treaty forces that landed in Fenit on 2 August.

Left: a pro-Treaty convoy passes through a village in the south-west. Improvisation was the order of the day, as seen by the two soldiers in civilian clothing on the commandeered fuel truck which is followed by an armoured Lancia. The soldiers are offered cigarettes by a local supporter.

After the start of the Civil War, recruitment into the Provisional Government army rapidly increased. As well as former IRA men, recruits included the unemployed and former members of the British Army. Many of the new soldiers initially had little training. In various southern campaigns, the ranks were stiffened by calling in the more experienced and disciplined Dublin Guards. Right: in what is most likely a barracks, is what was described as a medical unit. A miscellany of soldiers display equipment which includes what looks like two cylindrical mines (possibly captured), a stretcher, a tricolour, and curiously, a sock.

Right: military discipline was often easy-going in the newly-established Provisional Government army, as depicted in this 'Dublin Opinion' cartoon: Gent: "I wish to interview Lieut-General Michael J. O'Riordan, the Officer Commanding in this area'." Sentry: "Hey there, Mike, you're wanted!"

Left: another day, another town. A group of pro-Treaty soldiers, on campaign, march through an unidentified village. As the soldiers pass along this poorly-surfaced street, women observe. Gradually, from July 1922 onwards, Provisional Government control was established in towns across the State. However, in many areas, the Republicans remained in control of the surrounding countryside, adopting the tactics of guerrilla warfare.

Left: a rare image of captured pro-Treaty men. Under the eyes of their Republican guards, they play a football match at Swinford, Co. Mayo. As the pro-Treaty forces steadily captured more territory the number of Republican prisoners in captivity grew. By contrast, the Republican forces, who increasingly led a peripatetic guerrilla existence, without barracks to keep their prisoners, tended to let them go, on foot of a promise that they would not fight again.

Right: in the west, General Sean MacEoin's pro-Treaty forces, based in Athlone, had patchy control over areas in Co. Galway and South Roscommon. Here in Claregalway, in late July 1922, a group of Provisional Government soldiers assembles, with a Lancia armoured personnel carrier, complete with protective wire roof. The mix of uniform and civilian clothes reflects the rapid pace of army recruitment. Over the coming months, heavy skirmishes occurred in the west, notably in Mayo and Sligo.

Right: a posed group wearing a motley collection of helmets and caps (the man kneeling on the right has the characteristic soft-topped cap of the Provisional Government army). The caption of the 'Irish Independent' of 14 July 1922 describes: "A war scene in Co. Sligo. Riflemen entrenched behind a wall taking aim".

Left: a view from Mount Misery. Republican forces had occupied strongholds in Waterford City and raised the bridge over the River Suir. On 19 July 1922, Comdt-General Prout's forces set up a 18-pounder here on the escarpment to bombard the anti-Treaty defences in the city. Troops crossed in boats and seized the Quay. The bridge was lowered and the main force took the city.

Below left: the Post Office, on the Quay, was an important Republican stronghold and was directly shelled by the 18-pounder which had been moved to the opposite river bank.

Right: when Government troops reached the Granville Hotel on the Quay they discovered a mine in the hall and cut its wires. Here, in the portico outside the hotel, they proudly display the mine with a full roll of detonation cable and a hammer.
Below: the hotel today.

Further along the Waterford-Limerick defensive line, delineated by the River Suir, Carrick-on-Suir was controlled in July 1922 by anti-Treaty forces, comprising men from Waterford, Cork and Tipperary. This statuesque Republican volunteer, (left) complete with leather coat and ammunition pouch, guards the entrance to the Bank of Ireland in the town on 20 July. General Prout's troops converged on the town from Kilkenny to the north and from Waterford to the southeast. On 2 August, after an exchange of rifle and machine gun fire, the 18-pounder was brought into play and fired shrapnel shells at the defenders. In what had become standard practice, the anti-Treaty forces burned the local barracks and left the town, onwards to the next stronghold, Clonmel in this instance. Clonmel fell to the Provisional Government army on 9 August.

Right: Comdt-General John T Prout (1888-1969) seen here in Carrick-on-Suir on his arrival in early August. A native of Tipperary, he emigrated to the USA. In 1917 he joined the US 69th Infantry Regiment, which had links with the Young Irelander, Thomas Francis Meagher. (Coincidentally, Meagher was born in what is now the Granville Hotel in Waterford, seized by Prout's forces – see page 74.) He went with the 69th to France, part of the American Expeditionary Force. Seconded to the French Army, Prout was awarded the Croix de Guerre. Following his return to Ireland he became instruction and intelligence officer with the IRA in Tipperary. When the split occurred he was put in charge of the south-east campaign. He earned a reputation for excessive caution, and, in an internal army report, his command was criticised for indiscipline. Prout directed the successful action in April 1923 which effectively ended the Civil War. His troops mounted the sweep around the Knockmealdown Mountains in the course of which the anti-Treaty IRA Chief of Staff, Liam Lynch, was mortally wounded. Prout was demobilised in 1924 and returned to the USA.

At the end of July 1922, pro-Treaty forces advanced on the Republican heartland of South Tipperary. In one operation Commandant Padraig O'Connor skilfully led a successful action to capture Tipperary town. Above: O'Connor on horseback, flanked by two of his soldiers, after the fall of the town.

Left: the West Waterford IRA at Dungarvan Barracks.

As the war proceeded, abuse and propaganda flowed as freely as bullets.

Right: a constant theme of the pro-Treaty side was that those on the opposing side had not done much during the recent War of Independence, as was previously seen in the reference to 'trucers' chalked on the Lancia in Chapter 1. This pro-Treaty handbill makes the allegation that many of the Republicans were inactive in 1921 and emerged to fight only in 1922.

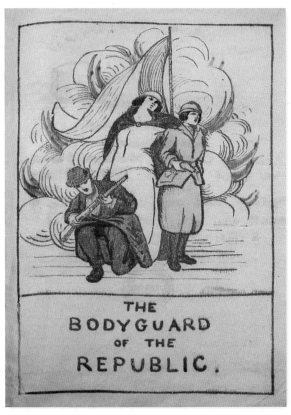

Right: Constance Markievicz produced a series of propaganda drawings supporting the Republican side on cyclostyled paper and had them posted around Dublin. Most were of a polemical and satirical nature, but this one adopts a more mystical theme, depicting male and female Republican fighters as 'The Bodyguard of the Republic'.

CAREY COLLINS — GO DOWN ON YOUR B----Y KNEES WITHOUT ANY MORE D----D
FUSS AND SWEAR ALLEGIANCE TO KING GEORGE AND HIS
HEIRS.

FAKER FITZGERALD — DON'T LISTEN TO DEVALERA.   I COULD TELL YOU A LOT
ABOUT HIS GREAT GRANDMOTHER AND SPANISH
GOLD.

THE BISHOP   — TAKE ANY OATH MY CHILD THAT WILL GET YOU OUT OF
YOUR PRESENT DIFFICULTIES.

COMIC COSGRAVE — IT WAS AN AWFUL JOKE TALKING ABOUT FREEDOM AND
REPUBLICS, YOU KNOW.

While the mainstream press, national and foreign, was universally pro-Treaty, a type of 'mosquito press' emerged on the Republican side. 'Poblacht na hÉireann, War News' was produced, during the second half of 1922, in the Republican heartland near Ballingeary by the Cork-Kerry border. It was edited by Erskine Childers. Of the other anti-Treaty publications, the most professional was 'Poblacht na hÉireann, Scottish Edition', produced in Glasgow (top right).

Many were impromptu cyclostyled affairs, as evidenced by this selection, below right. Clockwise, from top left: 'The Fenian (War Issue)'; 'The Nation (Sovereign and Undivided)'; 'Freedom'; 'Straight Talk'; 'Nationality' and 'Republican War Bulletin'. Interestingly, all carry the strap "seventh year of the Republic", thus emphasising that, in their view, the Republic had not been abolished and was still in existence.

Left: another poster by Countess Markievicz. Here, Hibernia, represented by the bound maiden, is harassed in turn by: Desmond FitzGerald (Minister for Publicity, in Union-Jack waistcoat); Michael Collins; a plump Bishop and WT Cosgrave (in clown attire).

POBLACHT NA h-EIREANN. SCOTTISH EDITION
REPUBLIC OF IRELAND
Saturday, December 9, 1922   Price - Threepence

THIS IS WHAT THE TREATY GIVES YOU

A Charter of Freedom!

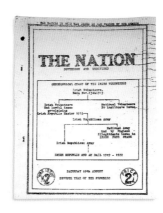

Left: happier days. Michael Collins with Harry Boland at a hurling match. Active in the 1916 Rising, Boland had been elected in the 1918 general election. He was appointed special envoy of the Irish Republic to the United States by de Valera. In 1922 he took the anti-Treaty side and thus was in opposition to his close friend Michael Collins. He was instrumental in persuading Collins to form the election pact with de Valera in May 1922. He gained a seat in the June 1922 election. After the Civil War started, he went on the run and into hiding in the Wicklow hills. The love triangle between 'Kitty' Kiernan, Boland and Collins was embellished in the 1996 film 'Michael Collins'.

Left: plaque at Skerries, Co. Dublin. Boland moved from Dublin to Skerries on 30 July where he checked into the Grand Hotel. At around 2 am the following morning, pro-Treaty troops burst into his bedroom. The unarmed Boland was shot and badly wounded in the abdomen – the exact circumstances have been disputed. Collins was concerned and asked that a 'good officer' go to the hospital to check on his condition. Boland died of his wounds on 1 August.

Erected In Memory Of Commdt. HARRY BOLAND T.D. Shot In This Area (Formerly The Grand Hotel) DIED 1st AUGUST 1922 National Graves Association

Right: the Imperial Crown of the Russian Crown Jewels, in all its splendour. There was an unusual Irish link with four of the more modest (diamond, ruby and sapphire) pieces of the collection.

As authorised by de Valera, a $20,000 loan was given to the new Bolshevik Government in October 1920. It was intended that this money would be repaid for the use of a future Irish delegation, when they arrived in Moscow. Pieces of the crown jewels were handed over as collateral in New York, by the USSR representive, Martens, to the Irish envoy Harry Boland (receipt, right). On his return to Dublin at the end of 1921, he handed the jewels to Michael Collins, but during an argument over the Treaty in January 1922 Collins threw them back at him saying, "Take them to hell" and "They're blood-stained, anyway!" As he lay dying in hospital, Boland asked his sister to keep them safe in the family home until de Valera returned to power and the Republic was established. Boland's sister handed over the jewels to the Government in 1938. They languished in a drawer in Government Buildings until they were returned to the Soviets in 1949, on receipt of $20,000.

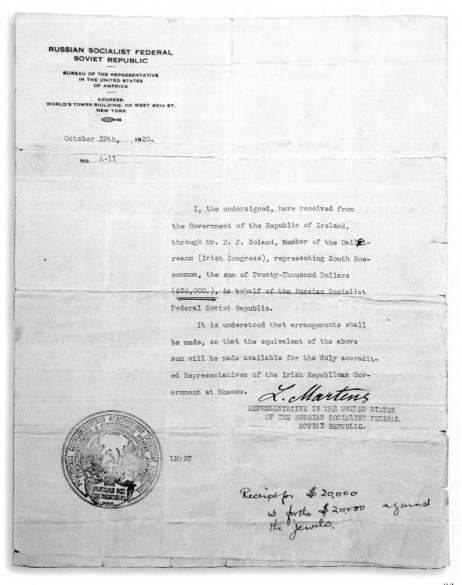

ARMOURED CARS PARTLY FABRICATED INCHICORE WORKS 1922

Above: the Provisional Government requested the GS&WR to upgrade Lancia personnel carriers at an early stage of the war. Here, four, partially fabricated, are lined up at Inchicore Railway Works. These Lancias were altered from the basic open-topped model, so as to have the roof enclosed by armour. The slope on the armoured plating allows for deflection of bullets or other projectiles. These upgraded Lancias garnered the name the 'Hooded Terrors'.

Left: a charabanc-load of the Tipperary IRA poses at Graignamanagh on 11 July 1922.

Right: members of the Civic Guard assemble for parade at Phoenix Park Depot. Established as an armed police force in February 1922, it was disbanded by the Provisional Government after a mutiny at the Kildare training barracks in May. A new Civic Guard was reconstituted in September. Remarkably, given the recent history of violence in the country, the new force was unarmed. It was initially deployed in pro-Treaty areas of the country, but was established elsewhere as the Provisional Government army gained control.

Right: indiscipline and drunkenness among their men was a worry for commanders of both anti- and pro-Treaty sides during the Civil War. Obviously Comdt-General Ennis had these concerns about his newly-fledged soldiers in the army of the Provisional Government when, in July 1922, he placed this warning in the newspapers that Dublin public houses could lose their licences for plying soldiers with (too much) drink.

Mac   Gift

IRISH REPUBLICAN ARMY,
H. Q. of 2nd Eastern Division,
Wellington Barracks,
27th July, 1922.

MILITARY ORDER.

The Officer commanding 2nd Eastern Division (which includes the County and City of Dublin) hereby warns all Proprietors of Licensed Houses that it is prohibited to supply members of the Irish Army in uniform with intoxicating liquor.

Where a member of the Irish Forces is found under the influence of drink in a licensed premises the licence of such will be immediately cancelled, and a fine imposed.

The closing regulations must also be enforced in future.

Signed (W. M. for)
T. ENNIS,
Commandant-General I.R.A.

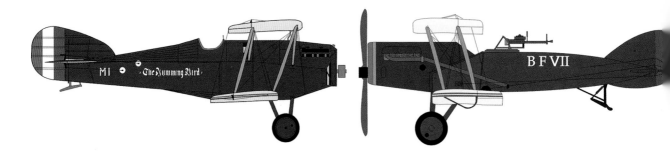

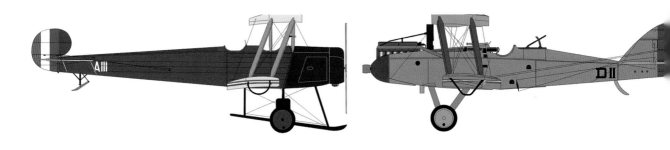

In November 1921, a Martinsyde Type A1 Mk II airplane, with a four-seat passenger compartment, was purchased in London during the Treaty negotiations, as a precaution in the event that an emergency departure by the Irish delegation became necessary. The plane was not required and was put in storage. It was later shipped to Ireland and re-assembled; it is pictured here (left) at Baldonnel, with the Irish tricolour being painted on its fuselage. Baldonnel (now Casement) Aerodrome was a former RAF base and became the headquarters of the Irish military aviation wing.

Left: the Army Air Service (to be known as the 'Army Air Corps' from October 1924) was established in mid-1922. It acquired its first fighter in early July. By the end of October 1922 there were 15 aircraft in service. Aircraft types soon included, from top far left, clockwise: Martinsyde F.4 Buzzard fighter (one of the fastest fighters of its time); Bristol F.2B fighter; DH.9 DII fighter and Avro 504K trainer.

Air Service fighters were extensively used during the south-west campaigns. As well as strafing Republican positions, duties included reconnaissance, patrolling railway lines and dropping propaganda leaflets.

Top right: at the RAF Museum at Hendon, a front-end view of the rotary engine of an Avro 504K. Regarded as an exceptional training aircraft, 8,000 of this type were manufactured in Britain during WW I.

Right: an Avro 504K trainer, seen here at Baldonnel Aerodrome. One of the first pilots, Lieutenant WP Delamere, is in the rear cockpit.

Right: planes of the Army Air Service at a public display in the Phoenix Park in August 1923, part of a ceremony on the anniversary of the death of General Michael Collins.

Above: a Bristol F.2B at Baldonnel. By the end of October 1922, the Army Air Service had acquired six of these fighters. This had been one of the most successful fighters during WW I. Interestingly, the Thomas Thompson Company in Carlow fabricated wing halves and wing spars for the F.2B during that war.

Left: a Lewis machine gun mounted on the rear cockpit of a F.2B fighter. Being buzzed by a fighter, followed by a stream of .303 bullets from the Lewis, was a frightening prospect for the Republicans on what now felt distinctly less than terra firma.

Chapter 4

By Sea & Land

With Munster and much of the west under Republican control, the generals of the Provisional Government army decided in July 1922 to mount a series of amphibious landings on the southern and western coasts. Steamers were commandeered and loaded with troops, armoured cars and artillery. Such landings could be perilous, but by dint of some planning, a poor strategic response from the Republican side and a lot of luck, they were all successful. With the taking of Cork in August, the core of the anti-Treaty 'Munster Republic' faded away. However, danger still lurked in the countryside, as happened when Michael Collins, travelling in a convoy through West Cork, was shot dead in an ambush on 22 August.

Óglaiġ na h-Éireann.

OFFICE OF ADJUTANT GENERAL,

General Headquarters, Portobello Bks.

BEGGAR'S BUSH BARRACKS

DUBLIN 16th. July 19 22.

9.30 p.m.

MY REFERENCE NO. Govt.No.4.

YOUR REFERENCE NO.

Please quote my number and date.

To: GOVERNMENT:

    SITUATION IN CORK: It is suggested from a Cork source that we should think of closing the Banks in that City having made arrangements whereby facilities could be given for dealing with the requirements of the larger firms.

    The attention of this Headquarter has also been drawn to the accompanying copy of the 'CORK EXAMINER' - It is the copy of Friday 14th July. It will be observed that the whole issue is entirely "Irregular" owing to the Censorship of our Opponents. It is a question whether the Cork Examiner should not be warned that it was guilty of a breach by a dissemination of false news, and that it would be liable for the ordinary penalties when conditions were restored to normal in Cork.

    The seriousness of the thing is that while we may accept the fact that the 'Examiner' is acting under duress it gives the Irregulars the advantage of its news service - A sheet published by themselves would not have this advantage..

Míceál O Coleam

COMMANDER-IN-CHIEF

Left: in this memorandum of 16 July, Michael Collins worries about Republican control of Cork. There was concern that the anti-Treaty side would seize the assets of the banks in the city. One worry was that £80,000 in silver coin in the Provincial Bank would be seized if its presence were known. Another issue was that the 'Cork Examiner' was under general censorship and had to carry official bulletins from the anti-Treaty IRA, as well as provide column space for the output of the Republican Publicity Department, then directed by Erskine Childers, in situ at the paper.

Left: seaborne landings were seen as the way to establish Provisional Government control in the west and south-west. The first landing by the pro-Treaty army was here at Westport on 24 July 1922. It proved difficult – the steamer 'Minerva' was thought to be too long for the quay. The landing was successful at high tide. An armoured car was brought ashore with the assistance of the engine driver on the harbour dredger. On arrival, 400 troops spread out to capture towns in Co. Mayo. This provided useful experience of an amphibious operation and was a template for subsequent landings.

Right: the next landing occurred in the early hours of 2 August 1922. The 'Lady Wicklow', a cross-channel ferry of 80 metres in length and 1000 tonnes, had been requisitioned from the British & Irish Steam Packet Company. Sailing to Fenit Pier, Co. Kerry from Dublin, it transported 450 pro-Treaty soldiers, the 'Ex-Mutineer' armoured car (back in service after seeing action on the anti-Treaty side in the Four Courts siege) and an 18-pounder. The landing was under the command of Brig-General Paddy O'Daly. Fortunately for the newly-landed troops, a landmine under the timber viaduct, part of the long causeway to the pier, had been recently disconnected by employees of the local harbour company. There was heavy fighting during the advance to Tralee, which was taken that day.

Right: commemorating the Fenit landing, a year afterwards. Fifth from left is Paddy O'Daly (Brig-General, GOC Kerry Command in 1923). Immediately behind him is Colonel David Neligan (Intelligence Officer, Kerry Command). Both took part in the landing at Fenit. Colonel Padraig O'Connor is second from the right.

Above: Sammy's Rock commands the road between Fenit and Tralee. Republicans directed fire from here on the advancing pro-Treaty forces. They were dislodged with the help of the armoured car.

On reaching Tralee, there were fierce exchanges between the IRA and advancing troops. O'Daly's troops took the town by nightfall and established command in Ballymullen Barracks. Nine of his soldiers were killed in the fighting. Their bodies were transported back to Dublin on the 'Lady Wicklow'.

Left: IRA memorial at Caherciveen.

The pro-Treaty side was now effectively under military direction: a 'War Council' (composed of Generals Collins, Mulcahy and O'Duffy) had been announced by Collins at a Cabinet meeting on 12 July. He requested an official instruction, which was issued by the Government in the following days.

Right: Portobello (now Cathal Brugha) Barracks, headquarters of the pro-Treaty army, 7 August 1922. Tension is evident on the faces of the officers (General Mulcahy, centre right) as one of the most decisive manoeuvres of the war is organised. With land communications blocked, it was decided that the way to gain control of the Cork region was by sea. An expeditionary force was to make a landing in Cork Harbour, with simultaneous landings at Youghal and Union Hall. A flotilla of steamers sailed from Dublin's North Wall that day.

Right: Commander-in-Chief General Collins strides through Portobello (where he had his quarters) on 7 August. He had attended a Requiem Mass for soldiers killed in Kerry. Behind him is 14-year old Alphonsus Culliton, adopted as the mascot of the army following his rescue by troops from a skirmish in Co. Wexford.

Kenmare was taken by pro-Treaty forces when 200 men under Brigadier Tom O'Connor 'Scarteen' landed at the pier (above) on 11 August 1922, from the vessels 'Margaret' and 'Mermaid'. Left: the Carnegie Library and the National (now AIB) Bank, which the troops occupied.

To the memory of
Bric. Cen. Tom O'Connor
and
Capt. John O'Connor
of Kerry No. 2. Brigade National Army
who were killed at Kenmare
on the 9th September 1922

R. I. P.

A month later on 9 September, the Republicans attacked and retook Kenmare. Tom O'Connor 'Scarteen' and his brother John (right) were shot dead in their home on Main Street. (Above: their grave at Kenmare.) 130 prisoners were taken, but were soon released by their Republican captors. It took until 6 December for the town to come back under Free State control.

L.&N.W. S.S. "CAMBRIA" LEAVING HOLYHEAD HARBOUR FOR DUBLIN.

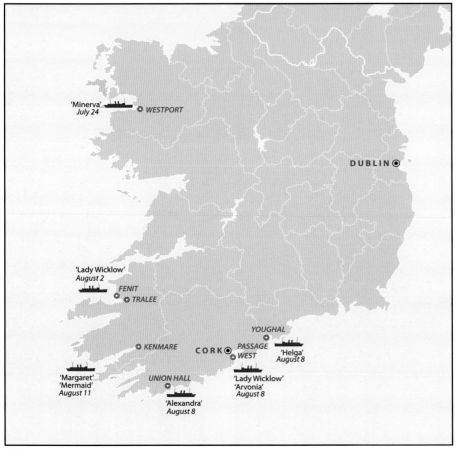

'Minerva'
July 24
◎ WESTPORT

DUBLIN ◎

'Lady Wicklow'
August 2
FENIT ◎
◎ TRALEE

YOUGHAL

◎ KENMARE
CORK ◎
PASSAGE
WEST
'Helga'
August 8

'Margaret'
'Mermaid'
August 11
UNION HALL
'Lady Wicklow'
'Arvonia'
August 8

'Alexandra'
August 8

Above: the cross-Channel ferry 'Arvonia' (previously the 'Cambria') was, along with the 'Lady Wicklow', commandeered by the Provisional Government for the landing in Cork Harbour. Displacing 1,800 tonnes, and launched in 1897, she was a London & North Western Railways steamer on the Holyhead to Dublin route. Around 100 metres long, with twin screws, she could travel at 21 knots. During WW I, she had served as an armed boarding vessel in 1914-15 and from 1915 as a hospital ship.

Left: amphibious ambition. The principal landings by pro-Treaty forces during the period July-August 1922.

Right: the crew of the L&NWR steamer 'Arvonia' were mostly Welshmen. Understandably, they were most reluctant to take part in the risky expedition to Cork. The Captain had advised Maj-General Emmet Dalton (in charge of the expedition) that, with mines laid in the Cork Harbour approaches, the mission was impossible. Here they prepare at North Wall in Dublin. As the Captain peers from the bridge, his second-in-command and seamen fix a protective mattress at the side.

Right: with a Provisional Government army officer in their midst, Captain Roberts (left) of the 'Arvonia' and his officers keep a close watch as a baulk of timber swings by. This may be to act as protection on the side of the ship, or to aid in unloading heavy military equipment during the landing.

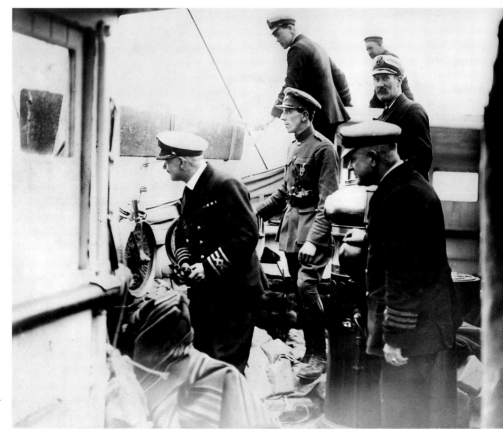

Above: on board the 'Arvonia', en route to Cork. Soldiers clean the 18-pounder gun. The scrawled letters on its protective shield show it is a veteran of the shelling of the Four Courts in June and of a brief and successful engagement on 4 July, against anti-Treaty forces entrenched at Millmount, Drogheda. It is Gun No. 10756, as per the 'Record of Rounds Fired' (page 38). Intriguingly, three civilians in the scene keep their heads down.

Left: posing for the camera, soldiers practise with their Lewis machine guns.

Above: in a poignant scene, soldiers dance on the deck of the 'Arvonia', to the tune of a melodeon-player, perched on the 18-pounder. For soldiers about to face the dangers of war, it was a way to pass the time on the long voyage south.

Right: unable to proceed upriver for fear of mines and sunken ships, the 'Arvonia' docked at the Queenstown Dry Docks, Passage West. (This had been the historic first landing point of Queen Victoria on her initial visit to Ireland in 1849.)

QUEENSTOWN DRY DOCKS
SHIPBUILDING
&
ENGINEERING C.
LIMITED

ESTABLISHED
1832
NAMED BY OUR GRACIOUS QUEEN ON HER FIRST
VISIT TO IRELAND AUGUST 6TH 1849
ROYAL VICTORIA DOCK YARD

Left: lifting off an 18-pounder at Passage West on 8 August. At around 1.3 tonnes weight, the ship's winches could handle this. A Peerless armoured car is seen here to the left. The unloading of this proved complicated as detailed below.

Below left: a reconstructed Peerless Armoured Car at the Curragh Military Museum. Armed with Hotchkiss machine guns mounted on twin turrets, and weighing nearly seven tonnes, this heavy vehicle was not suited for rough country roads.

During the landing at Passage West, in addition to the ship's winches, there was just a steam-powered dock crane. The combined force of these was insufficient to lift the Peerless from the ship. It was necessary to wait until the tide brought the ship to a suitable height. Using baulks of timber to provide a level passage, the armoured car was driven ashore, with the aid of the dock crane which relieved the pressure at the vehicle's front wheels.

Above: safely ashore, soldiers assemble at the dockside, about to set off on the journey towards Cork City, around 10 kilometres upriver. They were to encounter fierce resistance on the way. The Lancia armoured personnel carrier tows an 18-pounder across the crane tracks towards the dockyard exit.

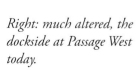

Right: much altered, the dockside at Passage West today.

Left: the scene today at the Passage West docks, looking at Great Island, across the west channel of the River Lee. As the 'Arvonia' disembarked its troops and equipment on 8 August, it came under Republican fire from positions across the water.

Left: bullet holes (circled) on the outer (western) wall of the Passage West docks, from what looks like a machine-gun burst from Republicans ensconced in the hillside above.

Right: fighting in the streets of Passage West in August 1922. Here a pro-Treaty officer, with revolver in hand, crouches as his troops shelter around the corner. The Peerless armoured car faces in the direction of opposing fire.

Below: a view from the heights above Cork Harbour. Republican forces rushed to the area to resist the incursion. There was heavy fighting amidst the rolling hills, fields and woods between Passage West and Rochestown in the days that followed the August landing.

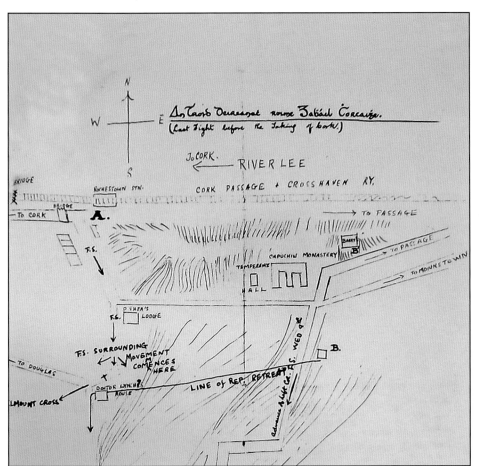

Above: the crossroads by the Capuchin College, Rochestown today.

Left: sketch map (by Fr Michael OFM Cap, an eyewitness) of battles in the area around the college. There were fierce engagements here on 8-9 August, as the Provisional Government army pushed towards Cork City.

Below: repairs to Belvelly Viaduct, south of Fota, on the Cork-Queenstown (Cobh) line, one of several railway bridges in the Cork Harbour area blown up in August 1922.

Above: Douglas Viaduct (now pedestrianised) of the Cork and Blackrock Railway. The Republicans blew up the three-span viaduct, to deny transit by rail to the city by the pro-Treaty army. Following fierce fighting on the approaches to the city, Cork was taken on the evening of 10 August, as the Republican forces withdrew.

Right: men of the Railway Protection, Repair & Maintenance Corps at work repairing Douglas Viaduct in early 1923. This was one of the biggest works they had undertaken.

Above: after the taking of the city, ships could sail upriver to berth at the Cork quays. Here in Lough Mahon, Upper Cork Harbour, care is taken in navigating past the 'Gorilla' (a steamer) in the foreground and, just visble, the 'No. 1 Hopper' (a dredging barge). These had been sunk by Republicans to prevent passage upriver.

Left: with what appears to be Generals Dalton and Ennis at his side, the captain of the 'Lady Wicklow' warns a passing ship of the dangers to navigation.

Above: the 'Lady Wicklow', laden with troops, in the upper reaches of Cork Harbour. Smaller and slower than the 'Arvonia', it had been commandeered from the B&I Steam Packet Company. Before its Cork duties, it had carried troops for the Fenit landing on 2 August.

Right: in the fighting during the approach to Cork City, pro-Treaty soldiers manoeuvre by the harbour-side, under fire. Two crouch in the back of 'The Manager' Rolls Royce armoured car.

Above: during their retreat, Republicans burnt Victoria (now Collins) Barracks. Locals salvage what they can carry from the burnt-out buildings.

Left: a Bristol F.2B fighter of the Army Air Service, in centre. On 10 August, Commandant Charles Russell flew BF No. 1 to Cork via Waterford. In his report he observed that all the Cork barracks were on fire. "Victoria Barracks was, in spite of the smoke and flames, a scene of great activity. Large numbers of men were moving about in a very excited manner."

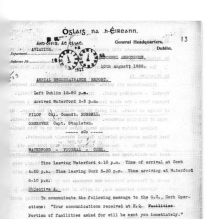

Above: Russell's Aerial Reconnaisance Report for 10 August. As well as the reconnaisance at Cork, he noted that Youghal was quiet and that the recently landed troops there were moving about freely. He distributed an impressive 4,000 copies of the army magazine, 'An tÓglach,' between Youghal and Cork City. He dropped a message for General Dalton – "Your communications received at HQ. Portion of facilities asked for will be sent you immediately." On the return journey, he came under heavy fire at Midleton and fired back for some minutes. It was a long day's flying, returning to Baldonnel at 9:15 pm.

Right: page of logbook of BF No. 1 for the period that includes 10 August.

Date.	Hour.	Pilot.	Passenger.	Route.	Time in Air.	
					hrs.	mins.
				Brought forward ...	188	35
2/8/22.	3.10.	Chas. F. Russell	Capt. Stapleton	Kilheany — .	2	15
7/8/22	11.35	Chas F Russell			1	30
10/8/22	12.55	Chas F Russell			1	30
10/8/22		Chas F Russell			2	.
10/8/22		Chas F Russell			2	
10/8/22		Chas F Russell			3	30
11/8/22		Chas F Russell			1	15
13/8/22		Com Gen McSweeney			1	30
6/9/22	11	Com Gen McSweeney			1	30
11/9/22		Com Gen McSweeney			2	15
12/9/22		" " "			2	15
24-9-22		Com Gen McSweeney			-	35
				Carried forward ...	210	40

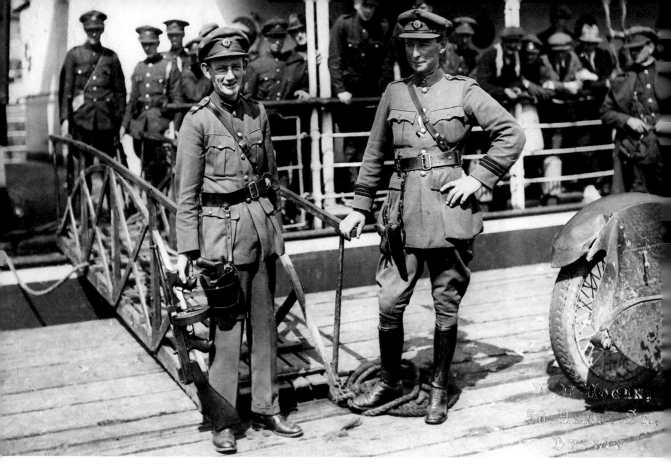

Above: the Provisional Government army was now in command of Cork City. At the gangplank of the 'Lady Wicklow', Maj-General Tom Ennis (with Thompson gun) looks relaxed. A more reserved-looking Col-Commandant MacCraith, is on the right.

Left: at Albert Street Railway Station, a soldier, surrounded by his watchful armed comrades, grasps a bundle of Lee-Enfield rifles on the back of a lorry. He is is distributing rifles to local pro-Treaty recruits. The 'Cork Examiner' describes the rifles as captured in the Douglas and Rochestown fighting.

W. D. HOGAN, 50. HENRY ST.

Above: in Cork, observed by a large crowd of curious onlookers, Provisional Government soldiers march captured Republicans off to captivity. As can be seen by the embossing, this series of images was taken by the commercial and press photographer, WD Hogan, who, with the army's approval, accompanied the ships on the mission to capture Cork.

Right: in this busy scene at Albert Street Station, soldiers mill around, with a Peerless armoured car in the background. A sandwich vendor finds a ready market for her wares.

111

Left: having taken Cork, troops took up positions at various strategic points. Here, soldiers guard a warehouse.

Right: closely watched by their captors, Republican prisoners say goodbye to their families at the quayside, as they wait to be transported on the 'Lady Wicklow' to Dublin for internment. This informal scene is evidence that the war was still in its 'civilised' phase, where captured prisoners were treated relatively leniently.

Left: soon after the takeover of Cork, it was alleged that a steamer, arrived from Hamburg, was carrying arms for the Republicans. This photograph shows troops and a Rolls Royce armoured car on the quays, ready to set off for the suspected ship. Nothing was found.

Right: during the period of de facto Republican control in Cork, the 'Cork Examiner' was under censorship and had to publish anti-Treaty communiqués. Before the Republicans withdrew from the city, they smashed the newspaper's printing press with sledgehammers.

Left: Cork 'Republican' silver. During July 1922 Cork was cut off from Dublin. The local silver-smiths, William Egan & Sons could not send silver to the Assay Office in Dublin. They devised their own unique marks, based on Cork's original marks of a ship between two castles.

Left: Cork 'Republican' stamps. During the anti-Treaty control of Cork, due to a shortage of stamps, a series was printed by the Eagle Printing Works in the city. These proclaimed the postal service of 'Po-blacht na hÉireann' (The Republic of Ireland).

Above: Chetwynd Viaduct on the West Cork railway was blown up by anti-Treaty forces, August 1922.

Right: IRA memorial in front of the entrance to Macroom Castle. On abandoning Cork City, Republican forces regrouped at the castle here. Seán O'Faolain described how the fighters had "fallen asleep where they stopped, on the grass, in motor cars, lying under trucks, anyhow and everyhow, a sad litter of exhausted men". They dispersed from here and the war in the south-west now entered a guerrilla phase.

Far left: as the reassuring news of the successful southern landings came, the Provisional Government was dealt a grievous blow. Arthur Griffith, President of Dáil Éireann, died on 12 August 1922 of a cerebral haemorrhage at the age of 51. Under strain and overworked, he had gone to a nursing home in early August, but had insisted on returning to work. Founder of Sinn Féin in 1905, this veteran of the nationalist struggle was one of the most eminent of the pro-Treaty leaders. He was much older than the rest of the cabinet and this gave him the cachet of an elder statesman.

Top near left: Griffith loathed Erskine Childers, calling him a "damned Englishman" in the Dáil. Yet, in his anti-Treaty 'Poblacht na hÉireann' of 14 August, Childers wrote graciously that Griffith was "the greatest intellectual force at stimulating the tremendous national revival".

Left: Michael Collins, Commander-in-Chief of the Provisional Government army, had just begun a tour of the south when news came of Arthur Griffith's death. Collins returned for the funeral. He marched in the funeral procession on 16 August. He himself had only six days left to live.

Right: bust of Michael Collins at his birthplace at Woodfield, near Sam's Cross, Clonakilty, Co. Cork.

Collins resumed his southern journey and reached Cork City on the night of 20 August. He spent the next day trying to trace Republican funds lodged in the city's banks. At 6:15 am on 22 August he set out for a long day's tour of West Cork, with the intention of assessing the situation on the ground and meeting old comrades. The party in the convoy consisted of a motorcycle outrider, a Crossley tender carrying soldiers armed with rifles and a Lewis machine gun, Collins with Maj-General Emmet Dalton in a yellow, open-topped Leyland touring car and, bringing up the rear, the 'Sliabh na mBan' Rolls Royce armoured car.

Right: on the morning of 22 August, IRA officers were upstairs in (the then) Long's public house, at the crossroads at Bealnablath (near Crookstown). Collins' party stopped here to ask a man (who happened to be an IRA sentry) standing outside for directions, at around 9 am. Anticipating that the convoy would return the same way, the Republicans decided to set up an ambush in a low valley, about a kilometre up the road.

Above: the Eldon Hotel, Skibbereen, West Cork, today.

Left: at around 4:30 on the afternoon of 22 August, General Michael Collins entered his Leyland touring car, as he left the Eldon Hotel in Skibbereen, where he had a meal. Amongst his meetings there, he met briefly the writer Edith Somerville, (whose brother Hugh, as it happened, was the Senior Naval Officer, Royal Navy, Queenstown, page 148) from nearby Castletownshend. This was the furthest point in his journey that day. The convoy embarked on the long and convoluted return journey to Cork City.

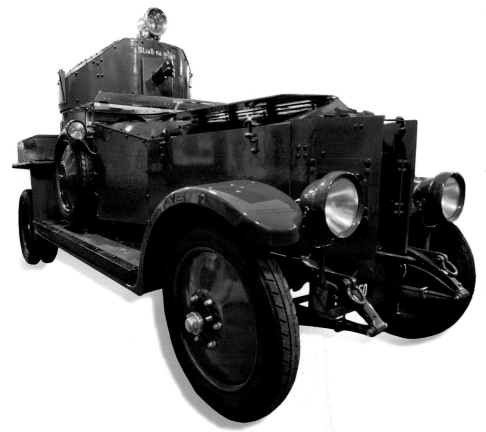

Left: with its potential for heavy firepower, the 'Sliabh na mBan' Rolls Royce armoured car was an essential component of the convoy on that fateful day. It is now maintained in pristine condition at the Military Museum in the Curragh.

Right: simple, spartan and effective. View inside the turret of 'Sliabh na mBan'.

Below right: the water-cooled Vickers machine gun of 'Sliabh na mBan'. During the ambush, it noisily raked the slopes around the attackers with withering bursts of .303 bullets. After the initial heavy bursts, the machine gun was only able to fire sporadically due to frequent jams – which the gunner had to clear. This was due to the unskilled reloading of the ammunition belt by an assisting inexperienced captain, present in the armoured car. Coincidentally, the gunner, a Scotsman, John McPeak, later deserted at Bandon, on 2 December 1922, and delivered the armoured car to Republicans. After some action in the Macroom area, the 'Sliabh na mBan' was hidden under a reek of hay at a farm in Gougane Barra. It was found, shortly afterwards, during a sweep of the area by pro-Treaty troops and towed back to Dublin. In 1923 McPeak was extradited from Scotland. He was imprisoned in Portlaoise prison and released in 1928.

12 Pages

12 Pages

Le Petit Journal

illustré

HEBDOMADAIRE
61, rue Lafayette, Paris

PRIX : **0 fr. 30**
3 Septembre 1922

Les convulsions sanglantes de l'Irlande

Au cours d'une tournée d'inspection dans le sud du Comté de Cork, Michaël Collins, chef du gouvernement provisoire de l'île libre, est attaqué par des rebelles en embuscade et, après une véritable bataille entre ceux-ci et les troupes de l'escorte, est tué d'une balle au front.

Left: "Les convulsions sanglantes de l'Irlande." In this imaginative illustration, 'Le Petit Journal' of Paris depicts the shooting of Michael Collins. The convoy, en route to Cork City, entered the ambush site at Bealnablath at around 7:15 pm, in light mist and fading light. The ambushers, lying in wait for hours, had given up on the convoy. A remaining few were about to clear away a barricade and a mine. After the first shot was fired at the convoy, Collins countermanded Dalton's order to get out of there, saying "We'll fight them". There was a heavy exhange of fire. Collins fired at the attackers with his Lee Enfield rifle, separated a little from his convoy. A shot rang out, and Collins fell mortally wounded, with a gaping hole behind his right ear.

Above right: Collins was lifted onto the rear of the 'Sliabh na mBan'. Later his body was transferred to the Leyland touring car. Following a nightmarish journey the party reached Cork City after midnight and the body was laid out in Shanakiel Hospital.

Right: haycart at the ambush site (marked X), soon afterwards. High ground is to the right. To the left, there is a stream and rising ground, from where the fatal shot was fired.

Left: memorial to Michael Collins at Bealnablath. He was aged 31 when he died.

Below: marker on roadside near where Michael Collins was shot.

Emmet Dalton managed, with difficulty, to send the news of the death back to Army GHQ, Dublin in the morning hours of 23 August. The message was relayed by shortwave radio to Waterville, cabled from there to New York, thence to Dublin by cable via London.

Collins' body was transported from Cork to Dublin on the cross-channel steamer 'Classic' and thence to the mortuary of St Vincent's Hospital (then located on the east side of St Stephen's Green.) Right: flanked by a guard of honour of nurses, senior officers carry the coffin down the steps of the hospital. The body was brought to lie in state at City Hall.

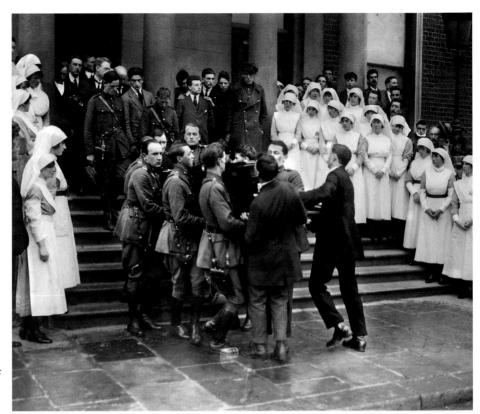

Right: in the Dublin City Gallery The Hugh Lane, 'Love of Ireland', painted later in 1922 by Sir John Lavery.

Above: Seán Collins mourns his dead brother, lying in state in the Rotunda of City Hall.

Left: with a gravedigger in the foreground, a group of officers salute at the funeral of Michael Collins, at Glasnevin on 28 August. There was universal sorrow at his death, even extending to the anti-Treaty side. According to Tom Barry, at the news of his death, around 1,000 Republican prisoners in Kilmainham Gaol kneeled to say the rosary for the repose of his soul.

Right: Shemus portrait of General Richard Mulcahy in the 'Freeman's Journal.' Not an outgoing personality, but energetic, methodical, efficient and ruthless, the Minister of Defence & Chief of Staff was now the military supremo and was appointed Commander-in-Chief of the army.
The other strong man in the cabinet, post-Collins, was Kevin O'Higgins, who represented a more civilian-oriented view of how the State should proceed and the two were to clash frequently.

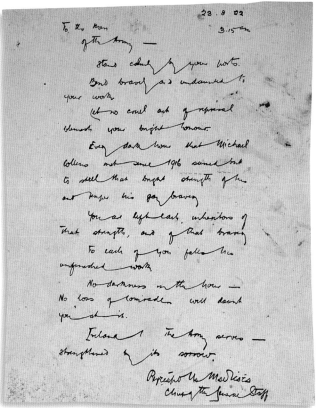

Right: early hours on 23 August Richard Mulcahy heard of Collins' death and at once wrote this message, as Chief of the General Staff, to the "Men of the Army". It starts: "Stand calmly by your posts. Bend bravely and undaunted to your work. Let no cruel act of reprisal blemish your bright honour...Ireland! The Army serves – strengthened by its sorrow."

Left: William Thomas (WT) Cosgrave replaced Michael Collins as Chairman of the Provisional Government. Given the paucity of administrative experience in the Cabinet, the skills acquired from his time in the Department of Local Government (established by the first Dáil) and Dublin Corporation were of benefit.

Below left: the Shemus cartoon, "Ireland's Via Dolorosa", in the pro-Treaty 'Freeman's Journal' of 24 August, captures the national grief. It places Collins in the pantheon of lost leaders from Wolfe Tone and Emmet, through O'Connell to Parnell and Griffith.

Below: amidst the grief was this instance of reprisal, as depicted in this poster attributed to Countess Markiewicz. A few days after Collins' death, two anti-Treaty Fianna youths were picked up at North Strand, shot and their bodies dumped at Whitehall.

"Father, Forgive them, for they know not what they do."
Sean Cole, Alf Colley
Boy Scouts of the FIANNA
Murdered aug 26. 1922.

Chapter 5

Mayhem on the Railways

Few people realise the full extent of the damage inflicted on the railway system during the Civil War. At that time the railways were perceived by Republicans as a very visible symbol of Government. As the war unfolded there were waves of destruction on the network – derailments and the wrecking of signal cabins, stations and bridges. One of the most spectacular examples was the blowing up of the Mallow Viaduct in August 1922. Railway engineers resolutely struggled to repair damage, aided from October 1922 by a special army corps set up to protect and repair the network. Due to increasing competition from road, railways had been in decline from their golden age – a decline which was hastened by the damage inflicted during the Civil War. The railways operating wholly in the Free State were merged to form the Great Southern Railways by 1925.

SHEMUS.

Left: when Shemus drew this cartoon of "The Wreckers" for the 'Freeman's Journal' of 28 April 1922, he had little idea of the extent of the devastation that was to be visited on the Irish railways. Initially, the IRA destroyed railways leading to the south to prevent pro-Treaty troop movements. Later, as the struggle moved to its guerrilla phase, the railways, a soft target, were sabotaged at will. Engineering Memo No. 5, from IRA GHQ (October 1922) put it clearly: "The systematic closing of roads and railways...is a work that should be carried out in a thorough and complete manner." On railways, it complained: "Press reports continually report the restoration of rail services... and in many bases there is apparent want of energy or initiativeness on the part of the Commands concerned to re-destroy them".

Left: rerailing a badly damaged locomotive.

Below: in what became a usual scene, a railway steam crane lifts derailed freight wagons .

The Provisional Government set up the Railway Protection, Repair & Maintenance Corps (RPR&MC) in October 1922 to guard the railways and repair damage. It was staffed by a mixture of soldiers and railway workers, and was under the command of Colonel Charles Russell (late of the Army Air Service, see Page 108).

Right: in the Cork area, in 1923, RPR&MC men, at a block post, overlook a works train.

Right: in 1922, Inchicore Railway Works became a veritable arsenal, producing armoured trains for the RPR&MC.

Right: an army marches on its stomach. A meal being prepared for men of the RPR&MC, engaged in repairing damaged bridges on the line to Queenstown (Cobh), by Cork Harbour.

Above: in Mullingar, an armoured train of the RPR&MC, with soldiers and crew. Note the sheep-dog next to the machine gun on top of the tender, to the left. 'Tutankhamen' reflects the discoveries in Egypt that were being made at that time.

Left: RPR&MC at sidings, Glanmire Road, Cork. In the background, is a camouflaged armoured works wagon and, in a siding in front of the locomotive, the 'Grey Ghost' (page 27).

Above: Inchicore Railway Works today.

Right: fitted out at Inchicore Railway Works of the Great Southern & Western Railway (GS&WR), an armoured Lancia, equipped with flanged steel wheels, which allowed it to travel on the rails (with top speed of around 70 km per hour.) The RPR&MC used these (including the 'Grey Ghost', below left) to patrol the railway network. Two of the series had turrets, as in this example. The works was the centre of engineering excellence in Ireland. It carried out armament work for governments of the time from WW I onwards.

Right: as shown on this map, damage to the GS&WR system by the end of December 1922 was: 375 incidences of damaged track; 255 bridges damaged; 83 signal cabins destroyed or damaged; 13 buildings destroyed by fire; 47 locomotives and rolling stock derailed or destroyed. There was also damage to the other railways such as the MGWR and D&SER. The mayhem on the entire network continued relentlessly into early 1923.

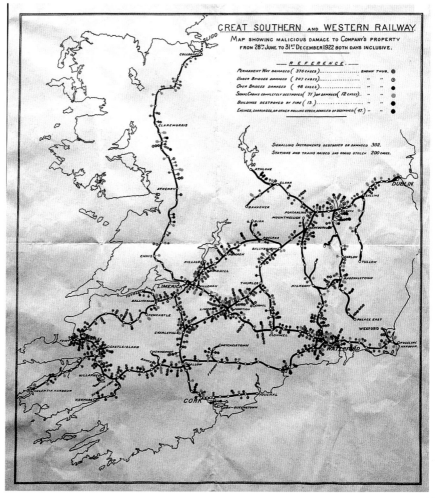

131

Above: a Cowans Sheldon breakdown crane, of the GS&WR, lifts a damaged locomotive, from the river at Foynes, Co. Limerick, April 1923. Essential for rescue work, these versatile steam-operated machines allowed for the lifting of heavy equipment on railway lines remote from road access. Irish Rail utilised similar steam cranes up to a decade ago.

Left: Dundrum, Co. Tipperary on the Dublin-Cork mainline on 1 December 1922. The steam crane is at work and a house-furnishing van is used to cart away damaged cargo.

Above: soldiers guard the scene at the derailment at Ballyragget, Co. Kilkenny in 1923.

Right: the 3 pm Limerick to Waterford wrecked at a bridge, February 1923.

Below: the GS&WR insignia.

Above: at Ballywilliam on 12 January 1923. Derailed locomotive No. 45 lies upside down on the embankment. The rescue crew pose for a photo. The railways had (and still have) effective procedures, equipment and capable trained staff who step in, recover derailed and damaged vehicles and get the track repaired and fit for traffic.

Left: derailed. The 4:30 pm Waterford to Carrick-on-Suir has come to grief on 10 February 1923.

Above: breakdown crane seized by Republicans and set on fire between Gowran and Bagenalstown on 14 January 1923.

Right: wagons jack-knifed near Newcastle West, Co. Limerick, on the GS&WR.

Below: Arthur Plumer, railway civil engineer, ex-amines a damaged bridge.

Centesimi 30

Sedici pagine

ILLVSTRAZIONE DEL POPOLO

ITALIA e COLONIE: Anno Lire 15 - Semestre Lire 8
ESTERO . . . . . » 30 » » 16
Si pubblica la Domenica

Supplemento della Gazzetta del Popolo

Anno III - N. 5   TORINO   4 Febbraio 1923

PER LE INSERZIONI rivolgersi esclusivamente agli
Uffici di Unione Pubblicità Italiana, piazza San Carlo,
via Santa Teresa, 2 - TORINO - ed alle sue succursali.

Un ponte ferroviario della contea di Tipperary in Irlanda, del quale i ribelli avevano fatto saltare un arco, è stato valicato senza danno, sopra le rotaie rimaste intatte, da un diretto sopraggiunto alla velocità di 70 Km. all'ora   *(Disegno di Alfredo Ortelli)*.

Above: speed was always the imperative for the railway engineers in getting the line back to service. Here, when an abutment was damaged, a quick solution was to prepare a crib made up of railway sleepers to prop the bridge.

Left: a wildly dramatic scene in Co. Tipperary, February 1923, as presented in the 'Illustrazione del Popolo'. In this depiction, anti-Treaty forces have demolished an arch of the multi-span railway viaduct. The express train, travelling at 70 km per hour manages to cross the damaged span.

Right: 'La Domenica del Corriere' shows a scene near Dublin, where Republicans derail a freight train and place it across the tracks, in the path of an oncoming train, in January 1923. It reports that eight passengers were seriously injured. This illustration is by the well-known Italian artist Achille Beltrame (1871-1945) of Milan, who also created works in oil, tempera and pencil.

Right: the burning of Waterford Goods Store

LA DOMENICA DEL CORRIERE

Anno . . . . . L. 10.— L. 18.—
Semestre . . . . » 5,50 » 10.—
Per le inserzioni rivolgersi all'Amministrazione del Corriere della Sera - Via Solferino, 28 - Milano.

Si pubblica a Milano ogni settimana
Supplemento illustrato del "Corriere della Sera,,

Uffici del giornale:
Via Solferino, 28, Milano

Anno XXV — Num. 3.   21 - 28 Gennaio 1923.   Centesimi 20 la copia.

Le prodezze dei ribelli irlandesi. Fermato un treno merci nelle vicinanze di Dublino, ne staccarono i vagoni, poi spinsero innanzi la locomotiva, senza macchinista nè fuochista, a tutto vapore. Ad una curva la locomotiva balzò dalle rotaie andando a piantarsi attraverso un binario parallelo. Poichè sopraggiungeva un treno passeggeri da Dublino, i ribelli imposero ai ferrovieri di non segnalare l'ostacolo. Il treno passeggeri cozzò quindi nell'oscurità contro la locomotiva deviata. Tre sue vetture andarono fracassate, ed otto viaggiatori rimasero gravemente feriti. Disegno di A. Beltrame.

Left: Wexford was taken by pro-Treaty forces in July 1922. However, a large amount of damage was subsequently inflicted on the railways in the county. Here, at the scene of a derailment on 15 August 1922, two rails had been removed. As it emerged from Killurin tunnel, along the banks of the River Slaney on the Dublin & South Eastern Railway (D&SER), the locomotive of the down Night Mail ran on the sleepers for over 150 metres before turning over. This isolated location was a favourite spot for derailments and ambushes. Republican activity continued strongly in Wexford, even into May 1923, despite the flooding of the area with Free State troops.

Left: the red-brick seven-span Taylorstown Viaduct over the Owenduff river, near Wellingtonbridge, on the Rosslare to Waterford line. In an attempt to isolate Waterford (then under anti-Treaty control) from attack, it was blown up in early July 1922.

Below: D&SER Insignia.

Right: the Rosslare to Waterford line suffered another blow in February 1923, this time by a very simple stratagem, without the use of even one stick of dynamite. The story runs that a young medical student of Republican persuasion rowed out, in a salmon skiff, to this control cabin on the central span of the Barrow Bridge. He unlocked the bridge and, with the small crown-wheel, hand-cranked the central span, to swing about its pivot into the open position, which allows shipping through. He then removed a single nut, removed the crown-pinion wheel and dropped it in the river. He rowed quietly back to shore. The central span could not be swung back into place and the line remained closed for the rest of the Civil War.

Right, and below: the majestic Barrow Bridge over the River Barrow near Campile. With 15 spans and at 650 metres in length, it is Ireland's longest railway bridge.

Above: Edenderry Junction on the Midland Great Western Railway. The down Galway Express was derailed on 17 February 1923. The carriages remain on the track, but the tender has spilled onto the embankment with the locomotive lying in the adjacent field.

Left: to the shed. A locomotive recovered from a wreck at Rathcurby bridge, on the Waterford-Limerick line in May 1923.

Below: MGWR insignia.

Above and right: Arma-geddon in a quiet corner of Co. Waterford. Ballyvoyle Viaduct was an impressive multi-arch masonry bridge spanning the River Dalligan, on the Waterford to Mallow line, originally opened in 1878. During the Civil War, damage had been inflicted on the viaduct in August 1922. More destruction occurred in January 1923 when the anti-Treaty IRA intercepted a ballast train and sent it backwards over the edge, as seen by the wagons hanging over the abyss.

Right: at Ballyvoyle, the GS&WR rescue team have sprung into action. The locomotive and other equipment were recovered by the ingenious technique of laying a temporary track from the base and around the side of the abutment, then back along the steep ascent up to track level. While the permanent way men adjust the temporary track at the top of the slope, a supervisor inspects the arrangements, before the battered tender is winched up.

Left: damaged locomotive No. 189 lies at the base of the abutment, as preparations are being made for its recovery.

Above: the rebuilt viaduct at Ballyvoyle on the (now closed) Waterford to Mallow line. Four steel lattice girders of 24-metre span rest on high concrete piers. It was faster to reconstruct using concrete and pre-fabricated steel than to reconstruct the original eight-arch masonry structure.

Right: locomotive No. 189 has been righted and is about to be hauled up.

Left: in early twentieth-century Ireland the railway system still constituted an essential economic artery. Localities suffered when a railway service was cut, not to mention a major blow to Ireland's infra-structure.

This was exemplified when the strategic ten-arch masonry viaduct at Mallow, which carried the Dublin-Cork mainline over the River Blackwater, was destroyed in August 1922. It caused great hardship across the region. A temporary station was put in place south of the river, with transfer by road to the station north of the river.

Below left: Mallow Viaduct today. It took only around 14 months to reconstruct it. Speed was of the essence at Mallow and, like at Ballyvoyle, a much quicker method employing spans fabricated in steel was used to replace the previous masonry structure.

Below: President WT Cosgrave, in the cab, as the train crosses on the ceremonial opening of the viaduct at Mallow on October 1923.

Chapter 6

Towards Endgame

Autumn 1922 was the beginning of the end. The Government (which became the Free State Government on 6 December) had captured the cities and was gaining control of the towns. Anti-Treaty fighters still roamed the mountains, particularly those of Kerry, Cork and Mayo. A cycle of ruthless executions of Republicans started in November 1922, which generated reprisals in return. The nadir came in early 1923 when the slaughter of pro-Treaty troops by a trap mine in Kerry led to the brutal murder of prisoners. As the anti-Treaty struggle ebbed away, Liam Lynch was shot on a lonely mountainside. The conflict juddered to an inconclusive end when Frank Aiken issued a ceasefire order to the IRA on 24 May 1923.

Soldier (to owner of late fruit stall): " Sorry, ma'am.   Nothin' for it but to put in your claim for compensation
Old Lady (sarcastically)|:   " Compensation !   If I'd a tin-opener, I'd get yeh out o' that before you deve
botulism."

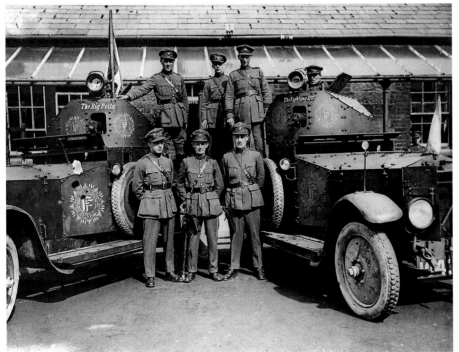

Above: cartoon in 'Dublin Opinion'.
Left: framed by the 'Big Fella' and the 'Fighting 2nd' Rolls Royce armoured cars, a group of officers poses in a Dublin barracks, July 1922. In the centre is Comdt-General Tom Ennis. He took part in key actions in Dublin and Cork. Rolls Royce armoured cars, and 18-pounder field guns, in ready supply from the British, were state-of-the-art weapons of the time. Their use gave the National Army a decisive advantage over the course of the Civil War.

Right: most of the participants in the Civil War were surprisingly young. Senior leaders such as Maj-General Emmet Dalton (Cork landings) and Ernie O'Malley (Deputy Chief of Staff, IRA), in mid 1922, were 24 and 25, respectively.

These two National Army soldiers seem scarcely out of their teens. Billeted in a rural cottage, they pose a little stiffly for the camera. If they are city boys, this glimpse of how people in the countryside lived probably came as a shock.

Right: as the Government took control of towns and cities, the anti-Treaty forces dispersed into the countryside. Despite the exigencies of guerrilla life, they maintained (to a greater or, more frequently, a lesser degree) a semblance of the organisational structure and practices of the IRA. This included training, as evidenced here in the latter part of 1922, where a Republican practises using a Thompson sub-machine gun at cliffs by the sea near Dungarvan.

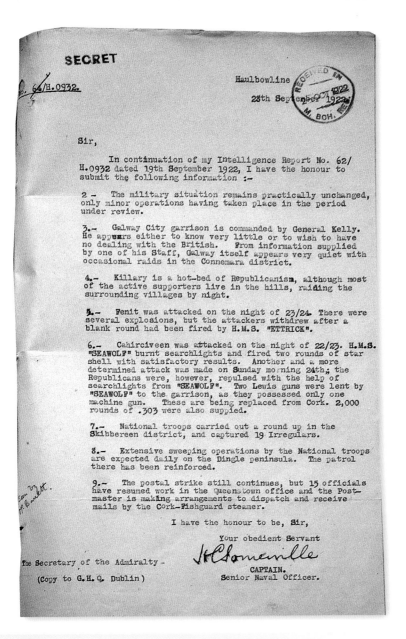

SECRET

No. 64/H.0932.

Haulbowline
28th September 1922

RECEIVED IN
OCT 1922
M. BOH.

Sir,

In continuation of my Intelligence Report No. 62/H.0932 dated 19th September 1922, I have the honour to submit the following information :-

2 – The military situation remains practically unchanged, only minor operations having taken place in the period under review.

3.– Galway City garrison is commanded by General Kelly. He appears either to know very little or to wish to have no dealing with the British. From information supplied by one of his Staff, Galway itself appears very quiet with occasional raids in the Connemara district.

4.– Killary is a hot-bed of Republicanism, although most of the active supporters live in the hills, raiding the surrounding villages by night.

5.– Fenit was attacked on the night of 23/24. There were several explosions, but the attackers withdrew after a blank round had been fired by H.M.S. "ETTRICK".

6.– Cahirciveen was attacked on the night of 22/23. H.M.S. "SEAWOLF" burnt searchlights and fired two rounds of star shell with satisfactory results. Another and a more determined attack was made on Sunday morning 24th; the Republicans were, however, repulsed with the help of searchlights from "SEAWOLF". Two Lewis guns were lent by "SEAWOLF" to the garrison, as they possessed only one machine gun. These are being replaced from Cork. 2,000 rounds of .303 were also supplied.

7.– National troops carried out a round up in the Skibbereen district, and captured 19 Irregulars.

8.– Extensive sweeping operations by the National troops are expected daily on the Dingle peninsula. The patrol there has been reinforced.

9.– The postal strike still continues, but 15 officials have resumed work in the Queenstown office and the Postmaster is making arrangements to dispatch and receive mails by the Cork-Fishguard steamer.

I have the honour to be, Sir,

Your obedient Servant

J.C.Somerville
CAPTAIN.
Senior Naval Officer.

The Secretary of the Admiralty -

(Copy to G.H.Q. Dublin)

Left: under the terms of the Anglo-Irish Treaty, the Royal Navy patrolled at will through Irish waters, In July 1922 there were two light cruisers and 11 destroyers on station – soon reduced after a crisis flared up in the eastern Mediterranean. On many occasions, the Royal Navy gave support to National Army troops in the south-west in 1922. Here, in a secret intelligence report to the Secretary of the Admiralty, Captain Hugh Somerville (brother of the writer, Edith Somerville), Senior Naval Officer, Haulbowline, recounts events along the coast, including how HMS 'Ettrick' fired a blank round at Republican attackers at Fenit on the night of 23 September 1922. He also tells how, on the night of 22 September, HMS 'Seawolf' gave assistance to the pro-Treaty garrison at Caherciveen, during an attack. Searchlights were shone, starshells fired and they provided ammunition, as well as two Lewis guns, to the defenders.

Left: Seen from Cobh, Haulbowline Naval Base. Under the Treaty, the British retained command of three naval ports including the base here and the coastal defences in Cork Harbour. The dockyard facilities were transferred to the Free State in 1923.

On 13 October 1922, an arrangement was made with a staff officer representing General WRE Murphy (then officer commanding Kerry Command) for cooperation with the Royal Navy during a planned drive on the Dingle peninsula. The staff officer passed on General Murphy's opinion that "for political reasons, the assistance of HM ships cannot be officially requested". It was agreed that a destroyer, on station off Valentia Island, was to listen on an agreed wavelength for the first five minutes of every even hour.

Right: the distinctive 'schloss-style' former RIC Barracks at Caherciveen, Co. Kerry, which dates from around 1875, now restored as the local museum. It had been burned during the Republican retreat from the town in August 1922.

Below: the destroyer HMS 'Seawolf'. She was completed in 1919 and based at Queenstown. 85 metres long, with a crew of 90, she was fast, with a top speed of 36 knots.

Left: Carrigaphooca Bridge, near Macroom, Co. Cork.

Left: memorial to Col-Commandant Tom Keogh and his six pro-Treaty army colleagues who were blown up by a trap mine near Carrigaphooca Bridge on 16 September 1922. There is also, on a nearby rock, a simple plaque commemorating a Republican prisoner who was brought here afterwards and shot, and whose body was put in the hole caused by the explosion.

Below: image of Tom Keogh, in bronze, on the monument at Knockananna, Co. Wicklow.

Right: memorial at the grave of Col-Commandant Tom Keogh (sometimes spelt 'Kehoe') in his native Knockananna. The sum of £600, a fortune at the time, was collected for this monument, which was unveiled in 1924, by (former) Comdt-General Liam Tobin. Keogh, only 23 at the time of his death, had been a member of Collins' 'Squad'. He had led the pro-Treaty expeditionary force which captured the Wexford area in early July 1922. Keogh was well commemorated elsewhere: Richmond Barracks in Goldenbridge, Dublin was renamed after him; two Rolls Royce armoured cars were named 'Tom Keogh' (formerly 'Danny Boy') and 'Knockananna', respectively, in his honour.

Below: figure of the dying Keogh, revolver in hand, on the monument at Knockananna.

Above: the conflict in the countryside had became a war of movement. Unlike their Republican opponents, the National Army had extensive access to cars, lorries, Lancias and armoured cars. With many railway lines sabotaged, motor vehicles were essential to get around.

Left: with the military patrolling the roads, the anti-Treaty forces resorted to ambushes, as this posed photograph of a phalanx of IRA men demonstrates.

Left: a wise soldier on campaign snatches a nap when he can. A sleeping soldier is stretched out in the front seat of a touring car. The can of petrol on the running board was necessary as there were few fuelling facilities.

Below right: a column of the anti-Treaty IRA in Sligo. Wrapped in their overcoats against the cold, they had to live in rough terrain, sometimes commandeering provisions. This unit is well armed, the section at the rear holding what look like Lee Enfields. The rest hold a miscellany of rifles.

The anti-Treaty forces were still able to inflict damage on their enemy. However, they had lost much territory and local support. The executions towards the end of 1922 severely affected morale. As the year ended, the pro-Treaty army, rapidly increased in size, had gained the upper hand in most of the country.

In October 1922, a Republican government was declared by anti-Treaty TDs, with de Valera as 'President of the Republic'. It was a paper exercise, quite remote from the realities on the ground, and wielded no control over Liam Lynch and the IRA.

On 13 July 1922, the IRA laid an ambush at Rockwood near Sligo, seized the 'Ballinalee' Rolls Royce armoured car and used it on forays in the area. Left: Christy MacLynn, driver, with the captured armoured car, now renamed 'Lough Gill'. Pro-Treaty forces mounted a large push on Sligo in September. The 'Lough Gill' was cornered in the lee of Benbulben on 19 July. The crew attempted to set it on fire, damaging the engine. Other Republicans hid at the southern base of the mountain that evening and fled up a gulley the next morning.

Above: four fugitives were captured by pro-Treaty forces on Benbulben on the foggy morning of 20 September and shot at this point marked by a cross, high up, overlooking Sligo Bay. These included Seamus Devins, TD, and Brian MacNeill, son of Eoin MacNeill. Two others were shot elsewhere on the mountain and it took two weeks to find their bodies. The slain Republicans are popularly known as the 'Sligo Noble Six'.

Right: the skeletal form of the roof trusses at Sligo Railway Station. It was attacked and burned out on 11 January 1923.

Left: 'Poblacht na hÉireann', 23 October 1922. Two days later, its editor, Erskine Childers, left for Dublin. He had been summoned by de Valera to be his new Minister for Publicity. Famous author, ('Riddle of the Sands'), and fervent Republican, the English-born Childers was not trusted by many. The pro-Treaty side had developed a phobia about him and regarded him as the eminence grise behind all major Republican 'outrages', such as the blowing-up of Mallow Viaduct. In reality Staff-Captain Childers had led a peripheral and peripatetic existence editing the paper, with the printing press being transported on a pony and trap between remote cottages in West Cork.

Left: the 'Limerick War News' of 11 August, 1922, produced by the pro-Treaty side, sets out, with vigorous enthusiasm, Childers' supposed villany.

Below: Beggar's Bush Barracks, Dublin.

The Civil War now entered a more bitter stage. The Third Dáil passed a draconian Public Safety Act at the end of September 1922. This included the power of execution for offences among which was the possesion of arms. It was first used when four IRA men (aged from 18 to 21) were found guilty, having beeen arrested with loaded guns in their possesion. They were shot on 17 November at Kilmainham Gaol. Allegations were made that these low-ranking youths were executed to establish a precedent for the execution of Childers, who had been captured seven days earlier.

Right: Erskine Childers was captured at his cousin Robert Barton's house in Co. Wicklow on 10 November. Ten days later he was brought before a military court, found guilty of being in possession of a pistol (a tiny automatic given to him by Michael Collins) and sentenced to death. He was executed at Beggar's Bush on the 24th. He shook hands with each member of the firing squad, and met his death bravely and with dignity.

Right: many prominent people pleaded for Childers to be spared. Jack B. Yeats sent this letter to the President. The scribbled comment demonstrates the revulsion felt for Childers.

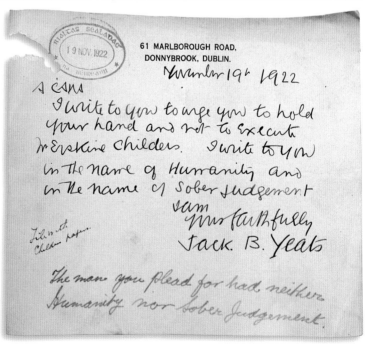

61 MARLBOROUGH ROAD,
DONNYBROOK, DUBLIN.

November 19th 1922

A Cara

I write to you to urge you to hold your hand and not to execute Mr Erskine Childers. I write to you in the name of Humanity and in the name of Sober Judgement.

I am
Yours faithfully
Jack. B. Yeats

File with Childers papers.

The man you plead for had neither Humanity nor sober Judgement.

ILLVSTRAZIONE DEL POPOLO

A Dublino il vice-presidente e un deputato della Camera irlandese sono stati assaliti da una banda armata che ha ferito gravemente il primo e ucciso il secondo a colpi di pistola

(Disegno di Alfredo Ortelli)

Executions continued, and this changed the IRA attitude to reprisals. On 27 November 1922, an alarmed Liam Lynch wrote to the Provisional Government protesting that "we on our side have at all times adhered to the recognised rules of war" and "every member of your body who voted for this resolution by which you pretend to make legal the murder of soldiers, is equally guilty." He gave notice that "unless your army recognises the rules of warfare...we shall adopt very drastic measures to protect our forces". Lynch issued an order on 30 November that "all members of the Provisional 'Parliament' who had voted for the Murder Bill" will be shot on sight. On 7 December, this was acted on when a member of the Dublin IRA shot dead Seán Hales, TD, and wounded Pádraic Ó Máille, Leas-Cheann Comhairle of the Dáil. (Depicted in this vivid illustration in 'Ilustrazione del Popolo', left.) The shooting took place as they were heading for the Dáil, having left the Ormond Hotel on Lower Ormond Quay. As it happens, a British armoured car was passing by and fired off some rounds at the attacking party as they escaped via Capel Street.

Right: Brig-General Seán Hales in 1921. He had taken a prominent role in the IRA in West Cork during the War of Independence. He was a friend of Michael Collins – they had been interned together in Frongoch in Wales after the 1916 Rising. He took the pro-Treaty side and was TD for Cork South. Hales had a meeting with Collins in Bandon on the fateful evening of 22 August 1922. His brother, Tom, was prominent on the anti-Treaty side and, ironically, commanded the IRA group that shot Collins.

Right. Seán Hales monument, Bandon, Co. Cork.

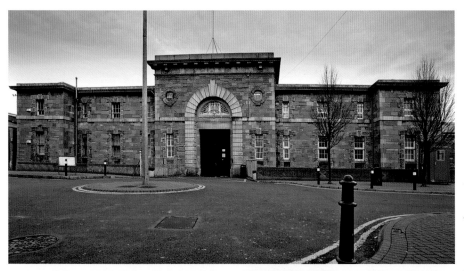

Left: Mountjoy Gaol, Dublin. Following Seán Hales' assassination on 7 December, the Executive Council met in an emergency session that evening. After some debate, it concluded with an order to execute, as a reprisal, four prominent Republicans incarcerated in Mountjoy Gaol. They had been captured after the taking of the Four Courts. The prisoners were roused from their cells the next morning at 3:30 and told that they were to be shot, as a reprisal, at 7:00 am. A firing squad shot the four together. The execution was conducted clumsily: nine revolver shots were required as coups de grâce. The prisoners had not been tried and these reprisal executions were not based on any law. Ernest Blythe, a Minister who had voted for the executions, later wrote: "I frankly regarded it as an act of counter-terror, not of vengeance, and though just, not primarily an act of justice but an extreme act of war."

Left: the executed four. Clockwise from top: Rory O'Connor, Joe McKelvey, Liam Mellows, Dick Barrett. Mellows, a socialist, was one of the few leaders, on either side of the Treaty divide, who had tried to articulate what an Irish Republic might actually comprise.

Above: cruel irony. Rory O'Connor (on the right) was best man at Kevin O'Higgins' wedding, in October 1921. Eamon de Valera is standing on the left. O'Higgins, as Minister for Justice, was one of the Executive Council that approved the executions, although accounts say that he initially hesitated.

Right: Mellows' last letter to his mother; outrage in the Scottish edition of 'Poblacht na hÉireann'.

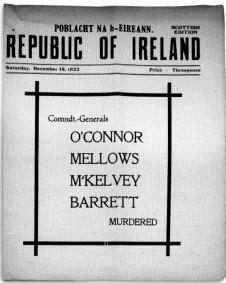

By early 1923, Free State forces had the upper hand and executions of captured Republicans continued. There was a wave of retaliation against prominent supporters of the Free State authorities. Amongst others, the houses of Sir Horace Plunkett at Foxrock and that of Stephen Gwynn (correspondent of the 'Observer') were burnt down.

President Cosgrave's house at Beech Park in Rathfarnham was set on fire and burnt down on 13 January 1923.

Left: Cosgrave inspects the remains of his house, surrounded by wary bodyguards.

Below left: the remains of pro-Treaty TD Seán McGarry's business premises, blown up on 1 February 1923. His house on Philipsburgh Avenue had been burnt on 10 December. His seven-year-old son, Emmet, died of burns received in the fire.

Below: Emmet McGarry.

Above: the Chief State Solicitor, Michael Corrigan's house on Leinster Road in Rathmines, was blown up on 29 January 1923. In a classic 'j'accuse' pose, the unfortunate gentleman surveys the ruins of his house.

Right. Palmerston House (near Naas, Co. Kildare), the seat of the Earl of Mayo (a Free State Senator), was also burnt down.

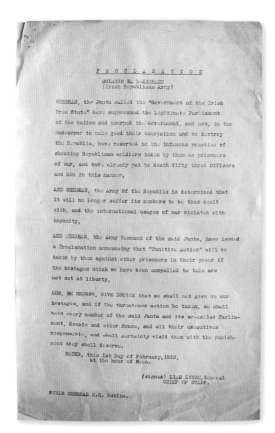

P R O C L A M A T I O N
OGLAIGH NA h-EIREANN
(Irish Republican Army)

WHEREAS, the Junta called the "Government of the Irish
Free State" have suppressed the legitimate Parliament
of the nation and usurped the Government, and now, in the
endeavour to make good their usurpation and to destroy
the Republic, have resorted to the infamous practice of
shooting Republican soldiers taken by them as prisoners
of war, and have already put to death fifty three Officers
and Men in this manner,

AND WHEREAS, the Army of the Republic is determined that
it will no longer suffer its members to be thus dealt
with, and the international usages of war violated with
impunity,

AND WHEREAS, the Army Command of the said Junta, have issued
a Proclamation announcing that "Punitive Action" will be
taken by them against other prisoners in their power if
the hostages which we have been compelled to take are
not set at liberty,

NOW, WE HEREBY, GIVE NOTICE that we shall not give up our
hostages, and if the threatened action be taken, we shall
hold every member of the said Junta and its so-called Parliament, Senate and other House, and all their executives
responsible, and shall certainly visit them with the punishment they shall deserve.

DATED, this 1st Day of February, 1923,
at the hour of Noon.

(signed) LIAM LYNCH, General
CHIEF OF STAFF.

FIELD GENERAL H.Q. Dublin.

Left: the temperature had risen, it was no longer an honourable war between former colleagues. On 1 February 1923, Liam Lynch, Chief of Staff, IRA, issued this proclamation. It notes 53 IRA men executed and the threat of punitive action by the Free State on prisoners if "the hostages that we have been compelled to take are not set at liberty". It warns the 'Junta' that they will not give up their hostages and if the threatened action be taken that all responsible will be visited "with the punishment they shall deserve".

Below left: memorial to Dr Thomas O'Higgins and his sons at Stradbally, Co. Laois. On 11 February 1923, anti-Treaty men called to the Stradbally house of O'Higgins, local doctor, County Coroner and father of Kevin (who would be assassinated in 1927). The raiders announced they intended to burn down the house, a scuffle ensued and Dr O'Higgins was shot dead.

Below: the principal inscription at the front of the memorial.

Right: after the blessing of the colours at Phoenix Park, President Cosgrave presents them to General McMahon, Chief of Staff, on the anniversary of the death of Michael Collins, August 1923. The Free State was strongly supported by the Catholic hierarchy. A joint pastoral issued by the bishops in October 1922 attacked the Republican side: "They carry on what they call a war, but which in the absence of any legitimate authority to justify it, is morally only a system of murder and assassination of the national forces".

Right: bitterness manifest in stone. '77' was generally known as the number of executions by the Free State in 1922-23. The Catholic church, Rathmines (opposite the then army GHQ) was rebuilt in the early 1920s. It appears that a mason, of presumably Republican sympathies, had placed the numbers '77' in lighter limestone, on the right of the lintel over the rear window.
Winston Churchill once said: "The grass soon grows over a battlefield, but never over a scaffold". The ruthless executions policy was effective. It secured the existence of the Free State, but at the price of subsequent decades of acrimony and division.

Left: during the early part of the Civil War, the Criminal Investigation Department (CID) was based at Oriel House on Fenian Street, Dublin. It was a shadowy quasi-military intelligence organisation. Founding members included those from Collins' 'Squad'. There are many allegations that the CID, facing the wave of Republican 'hit-and-run' attacks, resorted to a series of extra-judicial killings, in the period 1922-23, particularly in Dublin. Kevin O'Higgins acknowledged in the Dáil that CID members were not "plaster saints" but that they have "done great work for this State" and they "have broken the spinal column" of the conspiracy against it.

Below left: CID button.

Below: memorial at Upper Rathmines Road, to Thomas O'Leary, who was seized on 23 March 1923. His bullet-ridden body was found here the next day. St John Gogarty later wrote that O'Leary had led the IRA group which abducted him (then a Free State Senator) in January 1923.

Above: Noel Lemass memorial, in the lonely Featherbeds of the Dublin Mountains. Lemass (older brother of Seán, who later became Taoiseach) was abducted in broad daylight near Wicklow Street, Dublin, in July 1923. His badly decomposed body was found here three months later. A coroner's jury concluded that it was murder and that "forces of the State" had been implicated.

Right: Noel Lemass

Above and left: The cycle of atrocity and reprisal reached a new level of frightfulness in Kerry. It began at Bairinarig wood near Knocknagoshel on 6 March 1923. Lured by a false tip-off, a party of eight pro-Treaty soldiers, led by Lieutenant O'Connor (a local man, who was the subject of Republican animosity), came here to investigate a supposed Republican arms dump (on the left, now much overgrown). It turned out to be a trap mine. O'Connor and four others were killed, including two captains who were Dublin Guards, long-time comrades of Brig-General Paddy O'Daly, O/C Kerry Command.

Right: the Ballyseedy
Monument, by the Breton
sculptor, Yann Renard-
Goulet, unveiled in 1959.
What occurred here ranks
among the lowest points
of the Civil War. On 7
March 1923, the day
after the Knocknagoshel
trap-mine explosion, nine
prisoners at Ballymullan
Barracks were brought by
Free State soldiers to a barricade at Ballyseedy near
Tralee, ostensibly to clear
it. They were tied together
and then blown up by a
mine. Unbeknownst to
the troops, one prisoner,
Stephen Fuller, was blown
into a field and survived.
He was able to tell what
happened and, despite
efforts at a cover-up, the
news of the massacre soon
filtered out.

Below: detail on the
Ballyseedy Monument: a
chained foot.

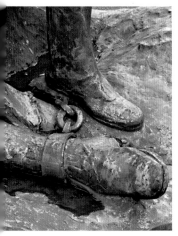

Left: memorial at Countess Bridge, over the railway line, near Killarney. The frightfulness continued: on the same day as the Ballyseedy explosion, soldiers of the Dublin Guards, stationed in the Great Southern Hotel in Killarney, brought five prisoners to this spot, again ostensibly to clear a barricade. Grenades were thrown and they were raked with machine-gun fire. Four prisoners died, one escaped.

Below left: on 12 March 1923, five prisoners were taken from the Baghaghs workhouse, near Caherciveen, by the Dublin Guards to a place nearby (memorial below). They were shot in the legs and placed on a booby-trapped barricade. The mine exploded and this time no one escaped – all five were killed.

Right: on 14 March 1923, Charlie Daly and three other prisoners (like Daly, two were from Kerry) were marched from Drumboe Castle, Co. Donegal (far right, now in ruins) and executed at this nearby sloping field (above). The prisoners had been tried the previous January, but no sentence had been imposed. Following the shooting of a Free State captain, an order to execute came by radio from GHQ in Dublin. Coincidentally, Stephen Fuller, the Ballyseedy 'escapee' had taken refuge in Daly's family home in Kerry, the day after the explosion.

**Meeting of IRA Executive
March 26 1922**

Above: a panorama of the isolated Nire Valley in Co. Waterford. An IRA Executive meeting in the area culminated in a vote here at Wall's Cottage (left, now demolished) on 26 March 1923, on a motion by Tom Barry, that continued resistance would not further the cause of independence. It was defeated by six votes (including that of Liam Lynch) to five. De Valera, also present, had no vote. Because of the divergence of opinion, the IRA Executive agreed to meet again. After the meeting, Liam Lynch exited the valley on the rough, boggy track via the Gap.

The Gap

Right: captured document showing proceedings of the 26 March meeting. Liam Lynch did not realise the game was up. Wildly optimistic, he thought that acquisition of mountain artillery from abroad would make all the difference. A month earlier, he had written that even "one piece of artillery...would completely demoralise the enemy and end the war..." Lynch passed through the Gap again around ten days later on his fatal journey, intending to travel to the reconvened meeting of the Executive at Araglin, Co. Cork, proposed for 10 April.

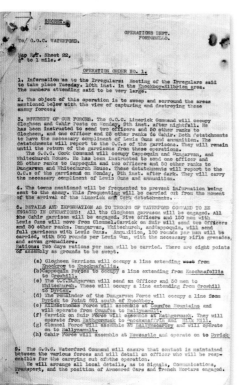

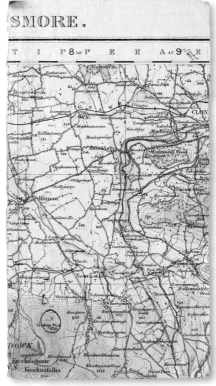

Above: death on bare mountain. The Liam Lynch Memorial in the Knockmealdown Mountains. In early April 1923, Liam Lynch, Chief of Staff, was en route, with his aides, to the planned meeting of the IRA Executive, to resume discussion on whether to continue the war. Pro-Treaty forces, acting on intelligence gathered by the CID, began a massive sweep of the Knockmealdown area.

Far left: detailed orders issued to the pro-Treaty troops for the round-up.

Near left: map used by troops during the operation.

On 10 April during the early morning sweep of the Knockmealdown area by Free State troops, Lynch and his companions were spotted escaping up over a ridge of Crohan West. Following an exchange of fire, he was felled by a long-distance shot at around 9 am. He was wounded in the abdomen and captured. Lynch was carried off the mountain with difficulty on an improvised stretcher comprising a greatcoat and rifles. He was eventually transported by ambulance to St Joseph's Hospital, Clonmel, where he died that evening.

Top right: guarded by four bronze Irish wolfhounds, the Liam Lynch Memorial. The 18m-high round tower was unveiled in 1935. With the heavy tree cover all around, it is difficult now to envisage the situation of the time, as described by one of Lynch's companions, Frank Aiken: "The fight took place on a mountain as bare as a billiard table."

Right: Liam Lynch's uniform that he was wearing when he was shot.

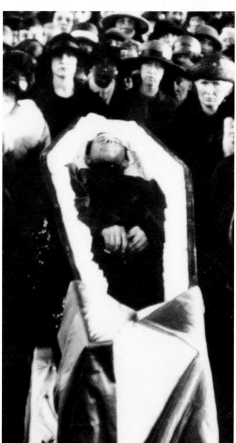

Far right: Lynch laid out in his coffin at Clonmel.

Small Cave

Above: the incident at the Clashmealcon Caves, on the north Kerry coast, was one of the most extraordinary episodes of the war. Six Republicans had gone into hiding at Dunworth's Cave. On 16 April 1923, pro-Treaty soldiers climbed down to search the cave. Two were shot, one dead and the other mortally wounded. From the cliffs above, the troops tried to flush out the Republicans, burning hay and turf, using machine guns, and, the following day, landmines, all to no avail.

Clockwise from far left: 'Aeroplane' Lyons; Lieutenant Pierson, National Army, mortally wounded on 16 April; memorial near caves.

Dunworth's Cave

As night fell, two Republicans attempted to escape and were drowned. The rest had retreated to the smaller cave, on the left along the cliff face. At midday on the 18th, the leader, Timothy 'Aeroplane' Lyons, surrendered, but the rope parted as he climbed up and he fell to his death. Accounts say that he was shot as he fell. The other three surrendered and were brought back to the barracks in Tralee, tried by military court and executed on 25 April.

Right: the last refuge. Smaller cave at Clashmealcon, and cliff which 'Aeroplane' Lyons attempted to scale (note small white cross at top of cliff).

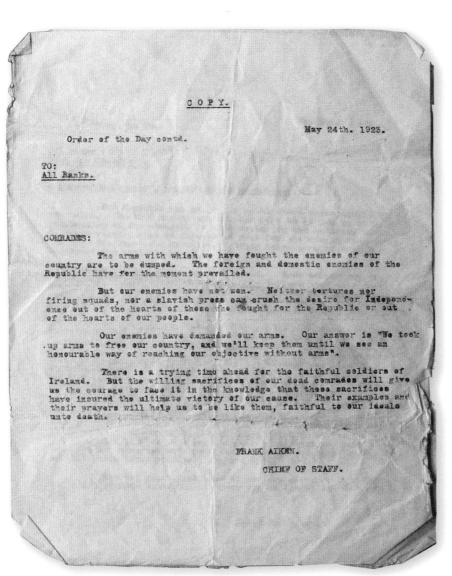

C O P Y.

Order of the Day contd.

May 24th. 1923.

TO:
All Ranks.

COMRADES:

The arms with which we have fought the enemies of our country are to be dumped. The foreign and domestic enemies of the Republic have for the moment prevailed.

But our enemies have not won. Neither tortures nor firing squads, nor a slavish press can crush the desire for Independence out of the hearts of those who fought for the Republic or out of the hearts of our people.

Our enemies have demanded our arms. Our answer is "We took up arms to free our country, and we'll keep them until we see an honourable way of reaching our objective without arms".

There is a trying time ahead for the faithful soldiers of Ireland. But the willing sacrifices of our dead comrades will give us the courage to face it in the knowledge that these sacrifices have insured the ultimate victory of our cause. Their examples and their prayers will help us to be like them, faithful to our ideals unto death.

FRANK AIKEN.

CHIEF OF STAFF.

Left: the end came swiftly. In little over six weeks after Liam Lynch's death, the new IRA Chief of Staff, Frank Aiken, in an Order of the Day (left), wrote that "The arms with which we have fought the enemies of our country are to be dumped. The foreign and domestic enemies of the Republic have for the moment prevailed." It was accompanied by a message from de Valera to the "Soldiers of Liberty – Legion of the Rearguard" stating that "further sacrifices ...would now be vain and continuance of the struggle in arms unwise in the national interest".

HARE PARK

For many Republicans, captivity was all that was on offer in 1923. At the end of the war there were around 12,000 in custody, in such locations as Hare Park Camp in the Curragh (left). With no negotiated peace and no handover of arms the Free State authorities were reluctant to release the prisoners. They were, in effect, hostages against a Republican resumption of hostilities.

Above: Republican prisoners pose outside the hut, chalked 'Bothán 15 Shligigh agus Mhuigheó ('Hut 15, Sligo and Mayo') at the 'Tintown' internment camp in the Curragh. Food was poor, sanitary conditions primitive and life monotonous. Many turned to education, but a few made efforts to tunnel out.

Right: Kilmainham Gaol was closed when the British left. It was soon re-opened to accommodate Republican prisoners. The last of these, Eamon de Valera, was released on 16 July 1924.

Right: a rare photograph of Eamon de Valera wearing a beard, useful when he was moving around the countryside, trying to avoid the, by now, victorious Free State forces. He shaved off the beard the night before the meeting (left) and his arrest in August 1923 at Ennis.

Left: with the IRA weak and exhausted, de Valera was able to better assert the political aspect of Republicanism. He proposed participation in the August 1923 General Election. On 15 August, he emerged from hiding to address a Sinn Féin election meeting at Ennis, Co. Clare. Shots were discharged and scuffles ensued as de Valera was seized by pro-Treaty troops and dispatched to prison. He was to spend around a year in captivity. The arrest is depicted here in the 'Illustrated London News' which carried the frothy caption: "The stormy petrel of Ireland caged at last".

Despite many of their candidates being incarcerated, the outcome of the election was surprisingly good for Sinn Féin at 44 seats. The pro-Treaty party in power, Cumann na nGaedheal gained 63 seats. Labour and others won 46.

Right: Richard Mulcahy, at an election rally, as depicted in a Munich newspaper.

Left: Women at work in the Sinn Féin HQ, Suffolk Street, December 1922. Unsurprisingly, it was the subject of many raids by Free State forces. Cumann na mBan presented a more public face of Republicanism during the war. Releasing imprisoned Republicans was a constant theme, as the posters indicate. Note the partial image of the 'Le Petit Journal' cover (opposite) in the middle poster on the wall.

Below left: a demonstration in Dublin by female Republican supporters. The bitterness in the aftermath of the Civil War is evident from the placards referring to executions and murders.

Right: in October 1923, there was a mass hunger strike by Republican prisoners which originated in Mountjoy Gaol. 'Le Petit Journal' depicts the strike sympathetically, comparing it with the fatal hunger strike (iconic in the nationalist struggle) of Terence MacSwiney, Lord Mayor of Cork in 1920. It depicts "nourriture abondante" being placed in front of the prisoners, to lure them from their intense resolution. To organise a hunger strike amongst thousands of prisoners was difficult. It broke up in disarray and was called off on 23 November.

12 Pages

12 Pages

Le Petit Journal

HEBDOMADAIRE
61, rue Lafayette, Paris

illustré

PRIX : 0 fr. 30
28 Octobre 1923

A l'Exemple du Maire de Cork

Quatre cent vingt-quatre Irlandais, enfermés dans la prison de Montjoie, à Dublin, s'étant vus refuser leur mise
en liberté, ont décidé la grève de la faim. En vain, les gardiens s'efforcent-ils de les faire céder en leur
présentant une nourriture abondante. Depuis le 14 octobre, les prisonniers s'entêtent dans leur farouche résolution.

Left: a suitable case for reconstruction. This is a view, from the dome area, of the rebuilding work underway on the eastern side of the Four Courts. The entire complex was in ruins, in the aftermath of shelling and explosions at the end of June 1922. The devastation is clear in this photograph. It shows scaffolding in place and masons busy at work.

Left: a present-day view, from inside the dome of the reconstructed buildings, looking east. The dome was rebuilt in reinforced concrete and then clad with copper. The reconstruction work was carried out in the period 1924–31, under the direction of TJ Byrne, principal architect in the Office of Public Works.

Right: the losers of the war. The defeated Republicans were liable to be arrested and were unlikely to have access to the meagre employment opportunities in 1920s Ireland. Emigration was the only option for many. Here, in 1923, are Republicans in Cobh. They commandeered this car at Dungarvan, and drove here, from where they are embarking on the SS 'Ausonia' bound for Canada.

Kevin O'Higgins gave the victor's version: he recalled the early days as "simply eight young men in the City Hall standing amidst the ruins of one administration, with the foundation of another not yet laid, and with wild men screaming through the keyhole". However, there was also a powerful empire across the water, on watchful standby, providing plentiful arms and ready to stamp out any hint of a Republic.

Right: Ministers of the Free State (in context, top hats were common formal attire in those days, O'Higgins is on left). This conservative group of men now had to face the task of reducing a swollen army and rebuilding a bankrupt, bitter and divided state. The Boundary Commission that followed, with the promise of border gains implied by Lloyd George in 1921, proved to be a damp squib.

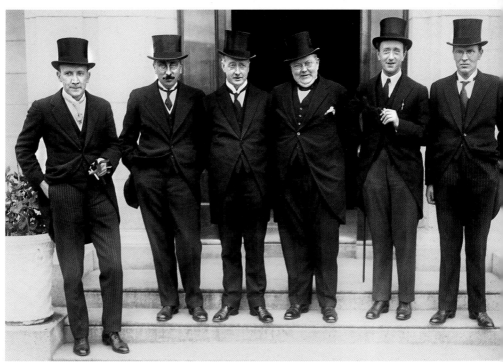

Since its beginnings in 1832 Glasnevin Cemetery has become a shrine for heroes of the national struggle.

The protagonists of the Civil War are now dead, remembered on plaques and headstones. Many of these former enemies now lie in close proximity, for all eternity, in Glasnevin. Clockwise from top left: the plaques, replete with a multitude of names, of the National Army plot; Kevin O'Higgins; Rory O'Connor; Erskine Childers; Eamon de Valera; Arthur Griffith; Cathal Brugha and, the most visited grave in Glasnevin, that of Michael Collins.

RICHARD TWOHIG † 17-11-1922
JAMES FISHER † 17-11-1922
RORY O'CONNOR † 8-12-1922

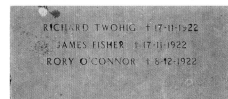

JOHN L. MURPHY † 30-11-1922
JAMES O'ROURKE † 13-3-1923
ERSKINE CHILDERS † 24-11-1922
MARY ALDEN CHILDERS † 1-1-1964

Bibliography

Archives Consulted:
Allen Library, Dublin.
Capuchin Archives, Dublin.
National Archives, Dublin.
Military Archives, Dublin.
British National Archives, Kew, London.
UCD Archives, Dublin.

Doctoral Theses:
Breen, T. M., *The Government's Executions Policy during the Irish Civil War 1922-1923*, NUI, Maynooth, 2010.
Linge, J., *British Forces and Irish Freedom: Anglo-Irish Defence Relations 1922-1931*, University of Stirling, 1994.
Ó Confhaola, P., *The Naval Forces of the Irish State, 1922-1977*, NUI, Maynooth, 2009.

Periodicals:
General Irish and British newspapers
The Defence Forces Magazine: An Cosantóir
History Ireland
Irish Historical Studies
Journal of the Irish Railway Record Society
The Irish Sword

Books:
Andrews, C. S., *Dublin Made Me*, Lilliput Press, Dublin, 2001.

Barry, M., *Across Deep Waters, Bridges of Ireland*, Frankfort Press, Dublin, 1985.
Barry, M., *Tales of the Permanent Way*, Andalus Press, Dublin, 2009.
Barry, T., *Guerrilla Days in Ireland*, Mercier Press, Cork, 1955.
Bateson, R., *Dead and Buried in Dublin*, Irish Graves Publications, Dublin, 2002.
Béaslaí, P., *Michael Collins and the Making of the New Ireland*, Phoenix Publishing Company, Dublin, 1926.
Borgonovo, J., T*he Battle for Cork*, Mercier Press, Cork, 2011.
Bowyer Bell, J., *The Secret Army: The IRA 1916-1979*, Poolbeg, Dublin, 1990.
Brunicardi, N., *Haulbowline, Spike and Rocky Islands*, Éigse Books, Fermoy, Co Cork, 1982.

Carroll, A., *Seán Moylan: Rebel Leader*, Mercier Press, Cork, 2010.
Casey, C., *The Buildings of Ireland*: *Dublin*, Yale University Press, New Haven and London, 2005.
Chambers, C., *Ireland in the Newsreels,* Irish Academic Press, Dublin, 2012.
Connell, J. E. A., *Dublin in Rebellion: A Directory 1913-1923*, Lilliput Press, Dublin, 2009.
Connolly, C., *Michael Collins,* Weidenfeld & Nicholson, London, 1996.
Coogan, T. P., *Michael Collins*, Arrow Books, London, 1990.
Coogan, T. P., *De Valera: Long Fellow, Long Shadow*, Hutchinson, London, 1993.
Cottrell, P., *The Irish Civil War 1922-23*, Osprey Publishing, Oxford, 2009.
Cronin, S., *Frank Ryan: The Search for the Republic,* Repsol Publishing, Dublin, 1980.
Curran, M., *The Birth of the Irish Free State 1921-1923*, University of Alabama Press, Alabama, 1980.

Deasy, L., *Brother against Brother*, Mercier Press, Cork, 1998.
Doherty, G., Keogh, D., ed., *Michael Collins and the Making of the Irish State*, Mercier Press, Cork, 2002.
Dolan, A., *Commemorating the Irish Civil War*, Cambridge University Press, Cambridge, 2006.
Doyle, T., *The Civil War in Kerry*, Mercier Press, Cork, 2008.
Doyle, T., *The Summer Campaign in Kerry*, Mercier Press, Cork, 2010.
Dorney, J., *Griffith College Dublin: A History of the Campus 1813-2013*, Griffith College, Dublin, 2013.
Dorney, J., *Peace After The Final Battle: The Story Of The Irish Revolution, 1912-1924*, New Island, Dublin, 2014.
Dorney, J., *The Story of the Irish Civil War*, Green Lamp Editions, Dublin, 2010.
Duggan, J. P., *A History of the Irish Army*, Gill & Macmillan, Dublin, 1991.
Durney, J., *The Civil War in Kildare,* Mercier Press, Cork, 2011.

English, R., *Ernie O'Malley: IRA Intellectual*, Oxford University Press, Oxford, 1999.

Farry, M., *The Irish Revolution, 1912-23, Sligo*, Four Courts Press, Dublin, 2012.
Farry, M., *The Aftermath of Revolution, Sligo 1921-23*, University College Dublin Press, Dublin, 2000.
Fanning, R., *Fatal Path: British Government and Irish Revolution*, Faber & Faber, London, 2013.
Fitzgerald, W. G., *The Voice of Ireland*, Virtue & Co., Dublin and London, 1923.

Garvin, T., *1922: The Birth of Irish Democracy*, Gill & Macmillan, Dublin, 1996.
Gillis, L., *Revolution in Dublin: A Photographic History 1913-1923*, Mercier Press, Cork, 2013.
Gillis, L., *The Fall of Dublin*, Mercier Press, Cork, 2011.
Greaves, C. D., *Liam Mellows and the Irish Revolution*, Lawrence & Wishart, London, 1971.
Griffith, K., O'Grady, T. E., *Curious Journey*, Hutchinson, London, 1982.
Gwynn, D., *The History of Partition (1912-1925)*, Browne & Nolan, Dublin, 1950.

Harrington, M., *The Munster Republic: The Civil War in North Cork*, Mercier Press, Cork, 2009.
Harrington, N. C., *Kerry Landing: August 1922*, Anvil Books, Dublin, 1992.
Hart, P., *The IRA and its Enemies: Violence and Community in Cork, 1916-1923*, Oxford University Press, Oxford, 1999.
Hart, P., *The IRA at War 1916-1923*, Oxford University Press, USA, 2005.
Hart, P., *Mick: The Real Michael Collins*, Penguin, London, 2006.
Harvey, D., White, G., *The Barracks, A History of Victoria/Collins Barracks, Cork*, Mercier Press, Cork, 1997.
Hayes, K., *A History of the Royal Air Force and the United States Naval Service in Ireland 1913-1923*, Dublin, 1988.
Henderson, W. A., *Souvenir Album of the Dublin Fighting*, Brunswick Press, Dublin 1922.
Hill, J. R., ed, *A New History of Ireland, VII: Ireland, 1921-84*, Oxford University Press, Oxford, 2010.
Hopkinson, M., *Green against Green, The Irish Civil War*, Gill & Macmillan, Dublin, 1988.
Horgan, J., *Sean Lemass: The Enigmatic Patriot*, Gill & Macmillan, Dublin, 1997.

Irish Air Corps, 1922-1997: An Official Souvenir, Air Corps, 1997.

Johnson, S., *Johnson's Atlas & Gazetteer of the Railways of Ireland*, Midland Publishing, Leicester, 1997.

Kennealy, I., *The Paper Wall: Newspapers and Propaganda in Ireland 1919-1921*, The Collins Press, Cork, 2008.
Keogh, D., *Twentieth-Century Ireland, Revolution and State Building*, Gill & Macmillan, Dublin, 2005.
Kissane, B., *The Politics of the Civil War*, Oxford University Press, Oxford, 2005.
Kostick, C., *Revolution in Ireland, Popular Militancy 1917-1923*, Cork University Press, Cork, 1996.

Litton, H., *The Irish Civil War: An Illustrated History*, Wolfhound Press, Dublin, 1995.
Lynch, C., ed, *From the GPO to Clashmealcon Caves*, North Kerry Republican Memorial Committee, 2003.

MacCarron, D., *Wings over Ireland, The Story of the Irish Air Corps*, Midland Publishing, 1996.
McCarthy, B., *The Civic Guard Mutiny*, Mercier Press, Cork, 2012.
McCarthy, C., *Cumann na mBan and the Irish Revolution*, The Collins Press, Cork, 2007.
McGarry, F., *Eoin O'Duffy: A Self-Made Hero*, Oxford University Press, Oxford, 2005.
McGowan, J., *In the Shadow of Benbulben*, Aeolus Publications, Manorhamilton, 1993.
Mac Guain, S., *County Wexford's Civil War*, Wexford, 1995.
McIvor, A., *A History of the Irish Naval Service*, Irish Academic Press, 1994.
MacSwiney Brugha, M., *History's Daughter*, O'Brien Press, Dublin, 2007.
Macardle, D., *The Irish Republic*, Merlin Publishing, 1999.
Macardle, D., *Tragedies of Kerry 1922-1923*, Irish Freedom Press, 2004.
Macready, N., *Annals of an Active Life*, Hutchinson, London, 1924.
Martin, K., *Irish Army Vehicles, Transport & Armour since 1922*, K. Martin, Dublin, 2002.
Maxwell, J., Cummins, P.J., *The Irish Air Corps, An Illustrated Guide*, Max Decals Publications, Dublin, 2009.
Maye, B., *Arthur Griffith*, Griffith College Publications, Dublin, 1997.
Mooney, T., *Cry of the Curlew: A History of the Déise Brigade IRA and the War of Independence*, De Paor, Dungarvan, 2012.
Morrison, G., Coogan, T. P., *The Irish Civil War*, Weidenfeld & Nicholson, London, 1998.
Morrison, G., *Revolutionary Ireland: A Photographic Record*, Gill & Macmillan, Dublin, 2013.
Mulcahy, R., *My Father the General: Richard Mulcahy and the Military History of the Revolution*, Liberties Press, Dublin, 2009.
Murphy, G., *The Year of Disappearances: Political Killings in Cork 1921-1922*, Gill & Macmillan, Dublin, 2011.
Murphy, S., *Comeraghs, Refuge of Rebels*, Kennedy Print, Clonmel. (n.d.)

National Graves Association, *The Last Post*, Dublin, 1932.
Neeson, E., *The Irish Civil War*, Poolbeg Press, Dublin, 1989.
Neligan, D., *The Spy in the Castle*, Prendeville Publishing, London, 1999.

O'Callaghan, J., *The Battle for Kilmallock*, Mercier Press, Cork, 2011.
Ó Comhraí, C., *Revolution in Connacht: A Photographic History 1913-1923*, Mercier Press, Cork, 2013.
O'Connor, D., Connolly, F., *Sleep Soldier Sleep: The Life and Times of Padraig O'Connor*, Miseab Publications, 2011.
O'Connor, E., *Reds and the Green*, University College Dublin Press, Dublin, 2004.
O'Connor, F., *An Only Child*, Macmillan, London, 1961.
O'Connor, U., *Oliver St John Gogarty*, Granada, London, 1981.
O'Donoghue, F., *No Other Law, the Story of Liam Lynch and the Irish Republican Army, 1916-1923*, Irish Press, 1954.
Ó Drisceoil, D., *Peadar O'Donnell*, Cork University Press, Cork, 2001.
Ó Duibhir, L., *Donegal & the Civil War, The Untold Story*, Mercier Press, Cork, 2011.
O'Dwyer, M., *A Pictorial History of Tipperary 1916-1923*, Cashel Folk Village, Co. Tipperary, 2004.
O'Dwyer, M., *Brigadier Dinny Lacey, by the men who knew him*, Cashel Folk Village, Co. Tipperary, 2004.
O'Dwyer, M., *Seventy Seven of Mine said Ireland*, Deshaoirse, Co. Tipperary, 2006.
O'Dwyer, M., *Death Before Dishonour*, Cashel Folk Village, Co. Tipperary, 2010.
O'Faolain, S., *Constance Markievicz*, Cresset Women's Voices, London, 1987.
O'Faolain, S., *Vive Moi*, Sinclair-Stevenson, London, 1993.
O'Farrell, P., *The Seán MacEoin Story*, Mercier Press, Cork, 1981.
O'Farrell, P., *Who's Who in the Irish War of Independence and Civil War, 1916-1923*, Lilliput Press, Dublin, 1997.
Ó Gadhra, N., *Civil War in Connacht*, Mercier Press, Cork, 1999.
O'Malley, C. K. H, Ó Comhraí, C., ed, *The Men will Talk to Me: Galway Interviews by Ernie O'Malley*, Mercier Press, Cork, 2013.
O'Malley, C. K. H, Horgan, T., ed, *The Men will Talk to Me: Kerry Interviews by Ernie O'Malley*, Mercier Press, Cork, 2012.
O'Malley, E., *On Another Man's Wound*, Anvil Books, Dublin, 1979.
O'Malley, E., *The Singing Flame*, Mercier Press, Cork, 2012.
O'Malley, M. C., *Military Aviation in Ireland 1921-45*, University College Dublin Press, Dublin, 2010.

O'Reilly, T., *Rebel Heart; George Lennon: Flying Column Commander*, Mercier Press, Cork, 2005.
Ó Ruairc, P., *Revolution: A Photographic History of Revolutionary Ireland 1913-1923*, Mercier Press, Cork, 2011.
Ó Ruairc, P., *The Battle for Limerick City*, Mercier Press, Cork, 2010.

Pinkman, J. A., *In the Legion of the Vanguard*, Mercier Press, Cork, 1998.

Quinn, J., *The Story of the Drumboe Martyrs*, McKinney, Letterkenny, 1958.

Regan, J. M., *The Irish Counter-Revolution 1921-1936*, Gill & Macmillan, Dublin, 1999.
Regan, J. M., *Myth and the Irish State*, Irish Academic Press, Kildare, 2013.
Reynolds, B. A., *William T. Cosgrave and the Foundation of the Irish Free State, 1922-23*, Kilkenny, 1999.
Riccio, R., *AFVs in Irish Service since 1922: From the National Army to the Defence Forces*, MMP Books, Petersfield, Hampshire, 2010.
Riccio, R., *The Irish Artillery Corps since 1922*, MMP Books, Petersfield, Hampshire, 2012.
Ring, J., *Erskine Childers, Author of The Riddle of the Sands*, Faber & Faber, London, 2011.
Ryan, G., *The Works, Celebrating 150 Years of Inchicore Works*, (n.p.), Dublin, 1996.
Ryan, M., *The Day Michael Collins was Shot*, Poolbeg Press, Dublin, 1998.
Ryan, M., *The Real Chief: Liam Lynch*, Mercier Press, Cork, 2005.
Ryan, M., *Tom Barry: IRA Freedom Fighter*, Mercier Press, Cork, 2012.
Ryle Dwyer, T., *Michael Collins and the Civil War*, Mercier Press, Cork, 2012.
Ryle Dwyer, T., *Tans, Terror & Troubles: Kerry's Real Fighting Story*, Mercier Press, Cork, 2001.

Share, B., *In Time of Civil War: The Conflict on the Irish Railways 1922-23*, The Collins Press, Cork, 2006.
Shepherd, E., *The Great Midland Great Western Railway of Ireland: An Illustrated History*, Midland Publishing, Leicester, 1994.
Shepherd, E., Beesley, G., *Dublin & South Eastern Railway*, Midland Publishing, Leicester, 1998.
Swords, L., *A Dominant Church*, The Columba Press, Dublin, 2004.

Taylor, R., *Michael Collins*, Hutchinson, London, 1958.

Valiulis, M. G., *Portrait of a Revolutionary, General Richard Mulcahy and the Founding of the Irish Free State*, Irish Academic Press, Dublin, 1992.

Walsh, M., *In Defence of Ireland: Irish Military Intelligence 1918-45*, The Collins Press, Cork, 2010.

Younger, C., *Arthur Griffith*, Gill & Macmillan, Dublin, 1981.
Younger, C., *Ireland's Civil War*, Fontana Press, London, 1986.

Glossary

Commandant	A military rank used in Ireland, equivalent to 'Major' in some other armies.
D&SER	Dublin & South Eastern Railway.
Free State	The state (known as the Irish Free State or in Irish *Saorstát Éireann*), a self-governing dominion of the British Empire, established on 6 December 1922 under the terms of the Anglo-Irish Treaty, replacing the (transitional) Provisional Government established in January 1922. Its remit covered 26 counties of Ireland. It existed until 1937 when, after a referendum, a new constitution, which replaced that of 1922, was approved. Ireland declared itself a republic under the Republic of Ireland Act 1948. This came into effect on 18 April 1949.
GHQ	General Headquarters.
GOC	General Officer Commanding.
GS&WR	Great Southern & Western Railway.
IRA	Irish Republican Army, which had its origins in the Irish Volunteers established in November 1913. After the split over the Treaty widened in January 1922, the forces on both sides continued to use the terminology 'IRA'. However, in July 1922 newspapers were instructed by the Provisional Government to describe its army as the 'National Army'. The present-day official title in Irish of the defence forces of Ireland is: *Óglaigh na hÉireann*.
IRB	Irish Republican Brotherhood. A secret society, prepared to use force to establish an independent Irish Republic, and which represented the continuation of the Fenian tradition. Michael Collins used his influence as president of the IRB to attempt to muster support for the Treaty. The organisation dissolved itself in 1924.
MGWR	Midland Great Western Railway.
O/C	Officer Commanding.
RPR&MC	Railway Protection, Repair and Maintenance Corps, established in October 1922, of the National Army.
TD	*Teachta Dála* (member of parliament, *Dáil Éireann*)
Treaty	The Anglo-Irish Treaty signed on 6 December 1921, by Irish plenipotentiaries and representatives of the British Government. It provided for the establishment of the Irish Free State. The northern Irish six-county entity had the option to opt out, which it immediately did.

Index